Media Rights and Intellectual Property

Media Topics
Series editor: Valerie Alia

Titles in the series include:

Media Ethics and Social Change
by Valerie Alia
0 7486 1773 6 (hardback)
0 7486 1771 X (paperback)

Media Policy and Globalisation
by Paula Chakravartty and Katharine Sarikakis
0 7486 1848 1 (hardback)
0 7486 1849 X (paperback)

Media Rights and Intellectual Property
by Richard Haynes
0 7486 2062 1 (hardback)
0 7486 1880 5 (paperback)

Alternative and Activist Media
by Mitzi Waltz
0 7486 1957 7 (hardback)
0 7486 1958 5 (paperback)

Media and Ethnic Minorities
by Valerie Alia and Simone Bull
0 7486 2068 0 (hardback)
0 7486 2069 9 (paperback)

Women, Feminism and Media
by Sue Thornham
0 7486 2070 2 (hardback)
0 7486 2071 0 (paperback)

Media Rights and Intellectual Property

Richard Haynes

Edinburgh University Press

Edinburgh University Press Ltd
22 George Square, Edinburgh

Typeset in Janson and Neue Helvetica
by TechBooks, India and
printed and bound in Great Britain by
CPI Antony Rowe, Eastbourne

Transferred to Digital Print 2008
A CIP record for this book is available from the British Library

ISBN 0 7486 2062 1 (hardback)
ISBN 0 7486 1880 5 (paperback)

Contents

Acknowledgements   vii

Part One: Theoretical issues in media rights

1 Introduction: understanding media rights   3
2 Intellectual property rights and the media   12
3 Copyright in the digital age   31

Part Two: Case studies in media rights

4 Music and copyright   47
5 Broadcasting rights to sport   67
6 Independent television producers and media rights   84
7 Celebrity and image rights   100
8 Intellectual property and the internet   113
9 Conclusion: media rights and the commons   131

Bibliography   144
Glossary   150
Index   160

Acknowledgements

I would like to thank the students who have taken my option on Media Rights as part of their studies for the MSc in Media Management in the Department of Film and Media Studies at the University of Stirling. Their varied and international backgrounds have broadened my understanding of intellectual property and its connection to creativity and media consumption around the globe.

I would like to thank my colleague Gillian Doyle for her support in helping me develop media rights as an aspect of my teaching and research, and also Philip Schlesinger, Simon Frith and Raymond Boyle for their general encouragement for this project. Finally, thanks to my editor at Edinburgh University Press, Sarah Edwards, for her initial prompt to write this book and her patience in seeing it come to fruition.

For Susan, Alice and Adam

Part One

Theoretical issues in media rights

1 Introduction: understanding media rights

In May 2003, a chance sighting of a feature article on Adolf Hitler in an edition of the 'middlebrow' magazine *Homes and Gardens* published in 1938 led to a global dispute over the ownership of a set of long-forgotten photographs of the Führer. Simon Waldman, the director of digital publishing at *The Guardian* newspaper, was intrigued by the '*Hello!*-style' article that appeared to celebrate the dictator's country lifestyle (Waldman, 2003). Wanting to share the revelation with a wider audience, Waldman scanned the article and posted it on his personal weblog (online diary). As news spread of the feature, the weblog saw a dramatic rise in traffic, with many readers worldwide posting messages with comments on the finding. Waldman decided to highlight the massive interest in the article to the publisher of *Homes and Gardens*, IPC Media, one of the UK's leading magazine publishers, with a view to finding out more about the feature and its origins. Waldman received a prompt response from the magazine editor citing copyright regulations and requesting the immediate removal of the scanned article from his website. Surprised by this tactic to suppress the article, Waldman removed the article but posted the correspondence with IPC on his weblog. Suddenly, the episode became the centre of a lively debate on international copyright laws and whether IPC had a right to prevent an article of such historical curiosity from being circulated on the Internet.

From correspondence to his weblog, Waldman discovered that the photographs used in the *Homes and Gardens* feature were not original to the article and had actually been in the public domain for many years. Waldman posted the article on his weblog once more. By this time, the scanned article had been copied and published on many more websites around the world, including the Wyman Institute for Holocaust Studies in Pennsylvania, USA. The Institute had lobbied IPC to facilitate the release of the article and admit that the magazine had colluded with Nazi propaganda prior to the Second World War. IPC issued a statement admitting the magazine's failure in the past and noting that the company was 'appalled' by the sympathetic coverage which *Homes and Gardens* had given to Hitler.

The entire episode is an allegory of the complex issues of copyright in the twenty-first century. It reveals the disruption and challenge to the hierarchical structure of established media industries that are premised in various ways on the control and exploitation of media rights. The reason for the disruption has been well documented in the analysis of new media technologies, namely the rise of digital media and networked communications that are globally accessible and instantaneously distributed. The fracas over the rights of publication also highlights the broader issue of how information circulates in a culture and what rights are attached to its availability and use. It further begs a question as to how we create things, in this case a weblog inspired by long-lost information of wider appeal. In many ways, access to and use of information and the motivations for creativity are central themes of this book.

Media Rights is not a book on legal practice and the law *per se*. Rather, it is about law and how it shapes certain aspects of the media industry. The book provides a guide to a part of media activity that is often hidden from the public gaze and absent from mainstream media studies. It is about aspects of media practice that are heavily dependent on the protection, exchange and enforcement of certain legal rights that broadly come under the heading of intellectual property. It is about the connection between cultural creativity and economics and how politics, power and the philosophy of property rights influence and shape the structure of the global media economy. It is also a book about how new media technologies are presenting immense challenges to age-old regimes of copyright and trademarks and how the contemporary media industry is coping with such dramatic change.

These are big themes that often require detailed observation and legal analysis. They are things that most students of the media have neither time nor inclination to investigate. If you wanted to study intellectual property in such detail, you would probably be doing a degree in law. Nevertheless, I do feel that the analysis of media rights has a place in the field in order to shed light on some of the most complex cultural issues of our time. For those studying law and interested in the media, the book aims to provide some understanding of how the media industry operates and how legal practice fits into the organisational activities of the media industry.

Because I do not expect everyone to be a master of law *and* a master of media analyses, the book is divided into two parts. Part One provides a focus on the rudiments of intellectual property law and how they relate to the media industry. This includes, in Chapter 1, a review of the basics of copyright, trademarks and patents and the regulatory regimes at the national and international level that sustain them, as well as other aspects of the law (in Chapter 2) that are important to understanding the subject. Understanding the basics of how intellectual property laws help shape the media industry then allows us to look at how changes in the industry itself are impacting on the shape and policing of these laws. Crucially, what has been euphemistically termed the 'digital dilemma' (National Academy of Sciences, 2000) now facing the regulation of copyright and related rights, that technology allows users to ignore such regulations, is brought into focus in Chapter 3. The process of digitalisation has had far-reaching effects on the structure of the media industries and has also transformed the legal mechanisms required to regulate it. In Chapter 3, I review the issues thrown up by new media technologies for the control and policing of intellectual property rights. Issues of control and power are at the heart of understanding contemporary struggles between governments, regulators, trade bodies, media corporations and consumers of media content. Understanding the connections between new media technologies, digital networks of distribution and new modes of carriage and consumption of media content are paramount in building our knowledge of what I am calling media rights.

Media-rights sectors

The issues raised by the process of digitalisation are being raised across all media sectors. To understand how copyright and other laws to protect intellectual property rights achieve their purpose, it is crucial to understand how different aspects of the media industry operate as technologies and businesses. Part Two focuses on specific areas of the media industry that have their own characteristics with regard to media rights. I have selected specific industry sectors that have undergone dramatic change in the past decade and have challenged the media-rights regimes that govern them. Each chapter reviews the specific structure of rights within each industry and reveals how copyright and other intellectual property rights govern their organisation and markets. Because the book is an introduction to the subject, and space for analysis is restricted, I have therefore added a series of related readings and websites at the end of each chapter. In this way, I hope that the book acts as a catalyst for further interest and critical thought among media-studies students and teachers alike.

More than any other media form, music has trailblazed the use of digital technologies and has undermined the copyright regimes that underwrite the recording industry. Chapter 4 begins with an overview of the complex beast that is music copyright. The analysis then turns to the music industry's contemporary struggle with digital distribution, such as its crusade to stamp out peer-to-peer networks. The chapter also addresses competing models of a revised industry that is at one and the same time increasingly fractured and diverse in the 'independent' sector as well as convergent and concentrated by major record labels that operate as part of the mass entertainment industry. Fears that piracy and the endemic decline in CD sales are throwing the industry into some sort of crisis are investigated and critically analysed.

Another sector of popular media content that has been transformed by emerging digital technologies is sport. In particular, the processes of digitalisation have opened up new vistas for the coverage of sport with dedicated sports channels, interactive television content and a multitude of dedicated sports websites. Often referred to as the 'king of content', sport has become of central importance to all forms of media. Specifically, in the UK and elsewhere, sport has gained immense significance in battles to control multichannel television. With this in mind, Chapter 5 briefly outlines how the marriage of sport and television in the UK has evolved and who benefits from this relationship.

Central to understanding the sport–television nexus are negotiations and bidding wars for both live and recorded highlights of sporting events. What is often at stake is the ability of specific sports to drive the uptake of new media technologies and pay-TV services. Sport, more than any other form of media content, has been used as a weapon to break into new markets, undermine competitors and ultimately dominate certain sectors of the media industry. The chapter reviews the spiralling cost of rights, in particular to football, and assesses the effect on both the sports and the broadcasting industries.

The chapter analyses the strategic decisions and motivation of broadcasters to acquire sports rights to drive the uptake of new digital channels. In particular, the collapse of ITV Digital and the debacle over the rights to televise the Football League represent a moment of crisis in the valuation of rights and an important conjuncture to analyse how rights are negotiated and licensed. The demise of ITV Digital led to further concentration of sports rights by the leading digital television platform BSkyB and emphasised the limitations of sport to drive new media businesses. In the UK context, the satellite broadcasters' unassailable position in the battle to control broadcasting rights to sport has driven European competition authorities to raise antitrust investigations into the market for rights. Chapter 5 analyses the political motivations for these concerns and the problems it raises for broadcasters and sports authorities alike.

Finally, the chapter raises the related issue of access to televised sport in the multichannel environment and critically analyses the political rationale for the protection of 'listed events'. The chapter concludes with an analysis of new media sport and the increasing convergence of media sports industries which is opening up new challenges for the exploitation of sports rights.

The sheer volume of multichannel television now available in those nations that have introduced digital broadcasting has presented new challenges to produce content to fill the broad spectrum of channels available. Popular programmes such as sport and movies that can eat up and fill many hours of dedicated programming on niche channels have certainly benefited from this new environment. Although sport and film services may be a key motivating factor for the take-up of multichannel digital television in many households, they are not the only forms of programming that win audiences. Historically, the US audio-visual industries have dominated the global market for programmes that has created a hegemonic position in the production of hit shows. Challenging this hegemony has led to a series of initiatives supported by European governments under the tutelage of the European Union as well as more proactive distribution activities by broadcasters and producers. The chapter critically addresses UK and EU legislation designed to support secondary markets and foster a competitive market for television production.

Chapter 6 investigates one of the great challenges for broadcasters and television producers for survival in the new broadcasting environment – the innovation of popular and potentially valuable programme formats. This may include formats that can be made to fit the tastes of specific national markets, such as *Big Brother*, or ready-made formats that are bought 'off the shelf' and adapted with minimum transformations, such as *Who Wants to Be a Millionaire?* Formats come with their own bundle of rights and licence agreements and have become the boom factor of the television industry. Interestingly, some of the most successful formats have come from traditional broadcasters such as the BBC. As multichannel television has eaten into the audience share of the UK's terrestrial broadcasters, they have sought to expand their operations both within pay-TV and beyond the UK in order to leverage new revenues and networks of distribution. Chapter 6 analyses the background to these developments, in particular focusing on the political and economic support from the UK government as it attempts to support audio-visual industries and create sustainable market conditions for a robust independent production sector.

The multichannel age has proved a boon to the independent production sector, although long-standing production practices by mainstream broadcasters have frequently undermined some of the potential growth of new creative talent. Here, the process of commissioning programmes has raised important issues regarding the influence and power of broadcasters in the television economy. Related to this is the issue of rights retention and exploitation, where the potentially lucrative sale of secondary and tertiary rights raises issues about rightful ownership of intellectual property and the balance of power in the television industry. Chapter 6 reviews the Communications Act 2003 that has introduced new terms of trade between broadcasters and independent producers, which serve to illustrate some of the complexities of media-rights ownership and licensing in an increasingly global television marketplace.

Another valuable commodity in the media industries are the people who attract the acclaim of critics and the adoration of fans – the personalities and stars of contemporary popular culture. Chapter 7 focuses on the rising cult of celebrity and how fame can be and is transformed into commercial success. One need only look at the way in which a cult figure like David Beckham has used his celebrity to endorse products and attract immense media interest to see how famous people become commodities. Like any product, there need to be regulations in place for how they are bought and sold. The chapter therefore examines the commercial control of image, or 'image rights'. Unlike the right of publicity in the USA, which enables every person to control the commercial use of his or her identity, or similar personality rights in other European states, image rights are not protected in any direct sense under British law. The chapter focuses on some of the philosophical arguments for and against rights in publicity before moving on to discuss ways in which stars have used the tort of 'passing off' or more formal statutes like trademarks to protect their commercial value in a media-saturated world. The important relationship between the use of contracts and certain proprietary rights is examined, as is the connection between image rights and laws protecting the privacy of stars in the media.

Issues of freedom of information and media innovation are at the heart of a raging debate on the relationship between copyright and the Internet. The digital distribution of media content has brought with it huge legal problems regarding the protection and management of copyright. Chapter 8 reviews the underlying principles of the Internet, in particular the concept behind the World Wide Web that provided a universal, non-proprietary standard for exchanging files and information. As critiques of the copyright regime have highlighted (Lessig, 2001; Vaidhyanathan, 2001), the expansion of statutory and technological controls on the transfer of copyrighted content on the Internet has started to have a detrimental effect on the creativity that characterised the Web's early development. The chapter critically reviews recent case law in the UK and the USA to provide a flavour of copyright in cyberspace and how contemporary legal battle-lines are being drawn between Internet libertarians and global corporate media industries. The theme of this chapter clearly connects with ongoing debates being addressed in other parts of the media industry – from the downloading of music, films and television programmes to the control of celebrity domain names and innovations in new media technologies. The interconnectedness of these themes is brought together in Chapter 9. The final chapter reviews once more the importance of rights issues in the study of the media industry. It proposes some new ways of balancing the relationships between creators, audiences and the media industry under copyright law, in particular the concepts of free media and the creative commons that are beginning to open up space for innovation and the sharing of ideas.

Why study media rights?

From the outline of the themes presented in this book, it is clear that intellectual property rights are at the heart of everyday activity in the media industry. This may not be immediately apparent to those involved in the media industries nor those who consume the vast array of products and services on offer from such a varied and culturally significant sector of our economy. But its cultural significance is perhaps the central reason for thinking about what media rights are and how they shape not only the media industry but also our lives. Media rights are the binding forces that hold the shape of our creative and cultural industries together – what John Howkins (2001) has referred to as our 'creative economy'. It is not to suggest that all forms of creativity have to have economic ends, for clearly there is a whole realm of creative activity that takes place outside the constraints of the market. Rather, it is to understand that more and more people earn a living from turning imaginative and innovative ideas into economic value. For that exchange to take place, something needs to help calibrate the economic value of creativity, which is where media rights come in. The value of rights to the creative economy is so great that some of the world's largest corporations lobby governments around the world long and hard to uphold their regulation and policing. Fissures in the regulatory regime of intellectual property caused by globalisation, changes in technology or shifting patterns of consumption such as peer-to-peer file-sharing bring to the boil public debate on such rights as they begin to touch upon people's everyday lives. As Howkins (2001: viii) suggests:

> Intellectual property used to be an arcane and boring subject, something for specialists only, but within the past few years it has become a powerful influence on the way everyone has ideas and owns them, as well as on global economic output.

The concept of owning ideas and information raises both political and philosophical questions. It raises political questions because it is the state that sanctions and regulates the rules by which intellectual property rights operate. It raises philosophical questions because the concept of intellectual property raises the issue of how best to organise the flow of information in society in order to generate new ideas and creativity. Indeed, the historical debate and ultimate structure of intellectual property regulations such as copyright have their roots in political philosophy. As we shall discover, different cultures around the world have different conceptions about how information flows through a society and how creativity might be rewarded. This has important consequences for media, at root a creative enterprise built on the circulation of information and ideas. Profiting from the control of ideas and information is therefore a serious business and one that increasingly employs massed ranks of lawyers to administer, as well as intrastate agencies and industrial watchdogs to police. To understand how media rights fit into the global media economy therefore requires knowledge of how media markets function, who the winners and losers are in terms of business and citizenship, and how economic might in the media industry often translates into political and cultural power. Increasingly, there is a concern that the balance in interests that intellectual property rights propose to regulate has been lost. That is, as the intellectual property systems of the state are gradually expanded, the rights of global media corporations are bolstered (along with their profits) at the expense of wider cultural innovation and the liberty of citizens (Lessig, 2001; Vaidhyanathan, 2001). Critics of the international creep of intellectual property that seeks to homogenise legislation on a global scale point to the hidden costs of this process. As Drahos and Braithwaite (2002: 4) persuasively argue, this threat is often covert:

> The danger to basic rights posed by intellectual property regulation is not an obviously visible danger. Rather it is a danger based on the quiet accretion of restrictions – an accretion hardly visible because it is hidden behind technical rule-making, mystifying legal doctrine and complex bureaucracies, all papered over by seemingly plausible appeals to the rights of inventors and authors and the need to encourage innovation.

What this suggests is that the argument over the efficacy of intellectual property rights is not necessarily that they are inherently bad but that, in the current climate of global media corporations, they are used in such a way as to actually inhibit innovation and creativity – in fact, the very thing they are supposed to foster.

How can this be so? One answer lies in the economics of the media industries and how it places barriers to entry for incumbent creators and innovators. This is why Part Two of this book is dedicated to case studies based on distinct areas of the media economy. Whether they concern music or the Internet, media rights play a central role in shaping the creative activity undertaken in these areas. Importantly, the influence of intellectual property rights cuts to the core of even the most mundane cultural experience. Investigating and critically examining why this should be so is the basis of this book. It is this seemingly inherent contradiction of intellectual property regimes that makes the topic of media rights both interesting and important for media scholars.

How to use this book

This introduction to media-rights issues is, as already noted, schematically divided into two parts. Part One provides an overview of the mechanics of intellectual property law and the contemporary pressures being brought by changes in media technology and new networks of communication. It provides the tools for understanding what is happening in specific parts of the media industry and how media rights operate within them that we focus on in Part Two. For those with a specific interest in particular sectors of the media industry, the case studies can be used as stand-alone chapters that inform analysis on your chosen topic. Further reading and study-related questions and websites help present a fuller picture.

Since I began researching and teaching in this area in the late 1990s, it is noticeable how quickly media rights have become a key issue not only in the media industry but in broader cultural politics. The court case involving the file-sharing service Napster has been the most visible manifestation of this heightened awareness. But it is not the only instance; and public interest has raised an eyebrow and begun to question the spread of intellectual property rights in many different areas of media activity. This is because the flow of information through society has implications for democracy and liberty, however defined, in different cultures across the world. By raising a flag to the moments of crisis and contestation in media rights, it is possible to analyse how and why things might be going wrong. Ultimately, I hope that the reader finds a more critical perspective on rights issues to be one that challenges the growing conventional wisdom that strong intellectual-property legislation necessarily leads to flourishing creative industries and a knowledge economy. If this book goes some way to conjoining students to these wider debates, I would be happy with that achievement.

2 Intellectual property rights and the media

But now we are facing a very new and a very troubling assault on our fiscal security, on our very economic life, and we are facing it from a thing called the video cassette recorder and its necessary companion called the blank tape. And it is like a great tidal wave just off the shore. This video cassette recorder and the blank tape threaten profoundly the life-sustaining protection, I guess you would call it, on which copyright owners depend, on which film people depend, on which television people depend, and it is called copyright.

(Jack Valenti, 1982, submission on Home Recording of Copyrighted Work: http://cryptome.org/hrcw-hear.htm)

Introduction

As any manager in a media business will tell you, getting a good media lawyer goes a long way to finding financial success. Why? Well, increasingly, the definition, control and exploitation of intellectual property is getting more central to the media's operation but harder to actually understand. The mention of copyright to many executives in the media industry often initiates a sharp intake of breath and a nod of resignation that it is a 'murky world' best left to legal experts. The boom in media law, particularly in connection with intellectual property, reflects broader shifts in the media marketplace and significant transformations in technology and methods of distribution. Law firms with specialist arms providing consultation and conveyancing in intellectual property are now commonplace and have become the cutting edge of legal practice in the media industry. In Chapter 3, we shall investigate in more depth the implications of digital technology and global networks for the media industries and copyright, but for now we shall concentrate on an overview of intellectual property rights, more specifically the underlying principles of copyright.

This chapter tells a story of the increasing use of intellectual property rights in the everyday activities of media organisations and how they have become the most important assets in media markets. It is well established that the media increasingly operate at the global level and that even localised markets are influenced by globalising processes. Intellectual property rights, in particular copyright, and its couplet with contract have become quintessential to contemporary media commerce and have their foundation in Roman law (Drahos and Braithwaite, 2002). As we shall see, although patents, copyright, trademarks and other forms of intellectual property rights were historically conceived to encourage individual creators by protecting their work, in the contemporary media environment they increasingly serve the interests of transnational corporations and the global business elite. Understanding what intellectual property rights protect and why they exist in their current form goes a long way to understanding how their meaning and function has changed to benefit the few over the wider public interest.

The chapter is organised around two sections: UK law and international law. It operates as a 'way in' to the legal debates surrounding intellectual property in order to allow the reader to engage with the wider theoretical arguments raised later in the book. The first section focuses on UK legislation, in particular the history of intellectual property rights and its justification, followed by a brief review of the most relevant legislation to the media industry – the Copyright, Designs and Patents Act 1988 and its subsequent amendments. We shall look at how this legislation applies to media industries, with a brief overview of its various constituent parts. The second section focuses on the creeping internationalisation of copyright. International treaties governed by the World Intellectual Property Organisation (WIPO) and the World Trade Organisation have had a significant influence on developments in copyright that have manifested themselves in new directives by the European Union, the most recent adopted by the UK in 2003. The section also compares and contrasts legislative developments in the United States, in particular the Digital Millennium Copyright Act 1998 that has raised serious alarm among information libertarians and small media businesses. The chapter aims to illustrate some of the contemporary complexities of copyright, patent and trademark laws and sets up the discussion of copyright in a digital environment in Chapter 3.

Copyright: philosophical underpinnings

Creators – authors, artists, inventors, designers, musicians, photographers, producers and directors – are entitled to exclusive rights to use and economically exploit their work. Media organisations might also be considered creators, and the state recognises the fact by providing legislative mechanisms to protect the publication, recording and broadcasting of related media content. As all legal textbooks tell us, patents, copyright, trademarks, design rights and rights in databases are based on *intangible* property rights. What does this mean? That, unlike 'real' or 'tangible' property such as land, intellectual property rights 'are rights given to people over the creation of their minds' (WTO, 2004). As such, intellectual property is based on an abstract object. However, given that we all have abstract thoughts all the time, how may intellectual property rights be known?

In copyright law, this problematic is commonly referred to as the idea/expression dichotomy. Basically, there is no protection in copyright for ideas. Rights are only extended to 'fixed', original and creative expressions, not the ideas upon which they are based. Extrapolating ideas from a book is one of the main reasons for reading a book in the first place. To prevent the subsequent use of the knowledge gained from the original source would seem absurd. Reproducing the physical manifestation of the book would, however, potentially breach copyright in the text. The fixed expression of the idea is therefore essential for copyright to subsist in a creation (usually referred to as a literary work). As we know, copyright does not only reside in published literary works; it may also exist in the fixation of sound recordings, video, film, computer memory, or any other retrievable format now available in the digital world. In the media industries, the distinction is important for those who would stake an economic claim in the creative process. If someone had an idea for a new television format but did not express the idea in a tangible form, such as writing it down, they would have no rights in a programme that used the same idea but had developed a treatment into a fully fledged programme. The only exception to this would be if the idea had been passed on in confidence – perhaps from the originator to an independent producer. A decision as to whether or not copyright had been breached in such circumstances would ultimately be decided in court based on the interpretation and application of the law by a judge.

The idea/expression distinction also throws up the issue of where the boundaries of intellectual property lie. Unlike tangible property, which may have clear lines of demarcation, intellectual property potentially knows no bounds. Indeed, some information in society circulates *ad infinitum* as part of an intellectual commons where anyone can use it and transform it at will. The main way in which intellectual property rights are bounded is by the repelling of challenges to those rights. Policing and protection of the copying, use and exploitation of intellectual property rights is therefore a key mechanism for society – largely led by business interests – to demarcate who owns what. Media corporations thrive on the private ownership of such intangibles as fictional characters, television formats and musical sounds to ensure that they have the exclusive right to exploit their commercial value. As we shall discover later in the chapter, the only other restriction on their rights to exploit a copyrightable work is time, as all copyrighted works have a finite longevity.

However, if intellectual property is locked too tight – behind prohibitive access or costs of use – then there is the threat that the general circulation of creative ideas in society may be blocked and innovation thwarted. In principle, copyright law attempts to prevent any monopoly of ideas. The general theory of copyright regimes around the world presupposes that the monopolisation of ideas would ultimately discourage people from creating new and original work. As Litman (2001: 13) neatly summarises, 'Authors are given enough control to enable them to exploit their creations, while not so much that consumers and later authors are unable to benefit from the protected work'. Copyright law therefore acknowledges that, in practice, all creativity is based on some prior knowledge or information that exists in the public domain. You would not be able to make a horror movie without knowledge of what a horror movie is and how its generic conventions work to build suspense and shock the audience. Making a horror movie requires that you use previous conventions in order that the audience understand what is supposed to be happening. The creative skill arises in the ways in which those conventions are adopted and reconfigured into something original. Creativity, then, does not occur in a social and cultural vacuum. It is constantly fed by previous experience, knowledge and understanding of what has gone before. Copyright walks a tightrope between balancing the needs of protecting authors' rights and the demands of a varied and innovative culture based on the free flow of ideas and information.

As we analyse different sectors of the media industry in Part Two, we shall discover that this balance is increasingly being tilted in favour of rights holders at the expense of the wider public, who demand freedom of information to help fuel creativity. This enclosure of knowledge is worrying because creativity in contemporary popular culture is increasingly based on the reassemblage and rearticulation of existing cultural artefacts. Increasingly punitive copyright laws put many cultural works out of bounds. As Drahos and Braithwaite (2002: 19) suggest, 'citizens

have been turned into trespassers in their own cultures'. We shall discuss the issues of freedom of information and its conflict with copyright
regimes later in the book. For now, it is enough to recognise how this
key principle of copyright has affected the way in which copyright legislation has evolved over time and how these principles have been exported
worldwide through international intellectual property-rights regimes.

At this point, it is worth noting how copyright is heavily connected with
economic theories of the market for information and how it operates. The
balancing act alluded to above presents the key problematic regarding the
economic distribution of information. Crucially, information is a public
good. That is, the marginal cost of consuming a unit of information is
zero. If I were to read a novel then pass it on to a friend who subsequently
passed it on to other friends, the additional cost of reading the book from
the original cover price would be nothing. This is the special feature of
information: it can be shared by two or by a million people at no extra cost.
The economic arguments for why authors should have ownership rights
of the works which they create are twofold. First, based on the political
philosophy of property devised by the seventeenth-century philosopher
John Locke (1988 edn), it is assumed that intellectual property rewards
the efforts of those who have created something original and have generally improved the stock of knowledge in society. Otherwise known as
the labour theory of intellectual property, it is an argument consistently
trotted out to defend knowledge ownership. Second, through personal
ownership of intellectual property rights, sanctioned by the state, markets
for informational goods can emerge and flourish. Again, it is argued that,
without such rights, not only would individuals not have the incentive
to create anything, but there would be no mechanism by which trade in
such informational goods could exist. James Boyle (2000b) suggests that
the problematic of informational economics that tries to find the best
way to distribute information efficiently as an economic resource is an
inherent contradiction of economic reasoning itself. Boyle argues that
the economist's desire to enable the most efficient circulation of information in a perfect market (where marginal cost is zero) runs contrary to
the monopolistic control of intellectual property rights, which is viewed
as being an essential incentive for authors, designers, producers or musicians to create. The problem, according to Boyle, is in the very premise
of the argument of a labour theory of intellectual property that panders
to industry demands for a legalised monopoly. In doing so, intellectual
property policy undervalues the welfare benefits of information circu-
lating in the public domain and exaggerates 'the role incentives have in
producing innovation' (Boyle, 2000b: 2,037). This is a theme to which
we shall return repeatedly through the course of the book. In the age

of digital media, the tension between the free flow of information and the private censure caused by the increasing depth, range and policing of copyright in particular is mounting and raising some serious issues about the future configuration of media practice and consumption.

Problems in claiming rights in ideas

There is some interesting case law to illustrate the reason why ideas are not copyrighted until they are 'fixed' in a tangible expression of some kind. In *Norowzian v Arks Limited and others* ((1998) 95(35) L.S.G. 37), the experimental film director Mehdi Norowzian claimed damages for infringement of copyright against the Arks advertising agency, Guinness Brewing Worldwide and Guinness plc. Norowzian brought his case after his technique of 'jump cut' editing to produce a surreal image of a man dancing was used in a landmark advertising campaign for Guinness in 1994. Although Norowzian's actual film was not copied, he sought protection in the technique of the film that he claimed represented a 'dramatic work'. The court ruled that although Norowzian clearly had a significant creative input into the editing procedure, his film did not constitute a dramatic work because the film was not capable of physical performance (a prerequisite of qualification for copyright protection). The case highlighted the difference between an idea and the material expression of a work, and illustrated that a technique or style of film-making does not constitute grounds for copyright protection.

It is this distinction that also allows parody of a work. So, when the comic duo Morecambe and Wise did their classic sketch of the Hollywood musical *Singin' in the Rain* (MGN 1952) in one of their Christmas Specials for the BBC in the 1970s, their interpretation of Gene Kelly singing the title song would have been deemed fair. This is because they had not used the original footage but merely copied the style of the film and its choreography. However, Ernie Wise's rendition of the song would have been deemed a public performance of the song, and royalty payments would have been due to the music publisher and possibly the composers of the song MGN, and Freed and Brown. This example brings us neatly to our need to understand what I am calling the 'bundle of rights' associated with copyright: the various rights that are associated with and assigned to literary and other media works.

Deciphering the bundle of rights

Copyright is made up of various rights to copy, all of which are exclusively held by the original owner until they are assigned to another party by being either sold or licensed to others. The bundle of rights includes reproduction, derivative works, adaptation or translation, broadcast, and public performance. These primary rights, which protect against 'primary infringement', are also accompanied by a range of rights to protect 'secondary infringement'. They include the unauthorised distribution and exploitation of copies, importation, rent for hire, exhibiting for public trade, and selling.

From this bundle of rights, we can appreciate how the infringement of copyright is relatively easy. All along the chain of production and distribution, the potential for copying or transgressing the rights of distribution is prevalent. For example, the practice of home taping has proved to be an area of infringement of reproduction, performance and distribution rights that has been a thorn in the side of the music industry. The bundle of rights is further complicated by the fact that any individual piece of work could have multiple claims to copyright. Take, for example, the following scenario presented by Robertson and Nicol (1992: 214):

> In the case, for instance, of a television documentary, there will be literary copyright in the script, dramatic copyright in the screenplay and musical copyright in any background music. The totality will be entitled to copyright as a film, and once aired will have a further rights as a television broadcast. One could also add to this any spin-out material or secondary rights such a book based on the documentary series or an accompanying website.

But these rights refer mainly to the commercial exploitation of copyrighted works. What about the use of media goods once they have been bought by the consumer?

Similarly, the ability to capture various forms of media on VHS video, DVD-RW, DAT, minidisk, CD-ROM, memory cards and a computer's hard disk means that issues are raised about private copying and personal use. Electronics manufacturer Sony caused a storm with the introduction of VCR machines in 1976. This led to one of the most-cited test cases in copyright history, *Universal City Studios v Sony Corporation*, often referred to as the 'Betamax Case', where the Hollywood giants sued on grounds of inciting unauthorised mass duplication of television programmes and films. In 1979, the District Court ruled in favour of Sony, stating that taping off air for home entertainment or time-shifting constituted fair use, a decision later ratified by the Supreme Court in 1984 after appeal by Universal and its Hollywood partners. History has shown that the technology actually benefited copyright holders and the film industry, who went on to make millions of dollars from the sale of rental and sell-through videos. When the electronics firm Amstrad introduced the twin cassette recorder in 1982, the music industry was in uproar that a technology had been devised that enabled multiple copying of one of its main carriers of commercial music. The music industry took action against Amstrad but ultimately lost on the grounds that tape-to-tape machines have other uses aside from copying prerecorded cassettes and that Amstrad had no control over the use of the machine once it had been bought. As we shall see in Chapter 3, the digitalisation of this process adds further complexities to who owns which rights and what constitutes infringement.

Copyright in perpetuity?

The question of how long copyrighted works should be protected brings us back to the wider question of balance in the flow of knowledge and culture in the creative industries. Copyright provides a limited period of protection which is nevertheless fairly extensive in its length. Under the Copyright, Designs and Patents Act 1988 and its amendment the Copyright and Rights in Performance Regulations 1995 (the 'Duration Regulations'), copyright in the UK lasts for the life of the author plus seventy years. The principle of providing a post-mortem period in the term of copyright is to allow the estate of the author or assignees to capitalise on the commercial value of the work. The length of the term of copyright and of other related rights has increasingly come under fire from advocates of freedom of information and the defenders of the public domain. The dispute focuses on the claim that copyright provides an effective monopoly on certain information that restricts the amount of works in the public domain and the flow of knowledge and information in society. The debate is put into stark relief when a particular term of copyright is extended, bringing works that were previously in the public domain back into the protection of rights owners. This occurred in the USA after the introduction of the Copyright Term Extension Act (1998), which extended an author's rights from life plus fifty years to life plus seventy years and corporate authorship from seventy-five years to ninety-five years. The extension, labelled the Sonny Bono Act after one of its leading advocates, the widow of musician Sonny Bono, effectively secured the protection of some of America's most prized cultural assets, including early Disney films of Mickey Mouse and the songs of George Gershwin. Proponents of the Act argued that extended life expectancy during the twentieth century warranted a longer term of protection and also brought the USA in line with the EU, which had harmonised the length of its copyright term under a similar EC Directive (1993). Critics of the Act pointed to the bias in favour of media corporations at the expense of the public at large and made a philosophical claim that extended protection would not necessarily serve to improve the level of creativity in the arts. Indeed, the argument that copyright is an essential impetus for authors to create new work is massively overshadowed by the need of existing copyright holders to maintain and expand the commercial value of their work.

Challenging the copyright term: Eldred v Ashcroft

In October 2002, the United States Supreme Court heard a case that challenged the Sonny Bono Act of 1998, claiming that it was against the Copyright Clause of the US Constitution. The case was based on a petition raised by online publisher Eric Eldred, who ran a website that enabled users to download various types of literature that had fallen out of copyright and were in the public domain, against the Attorney General of the United States, John Ashcroft, who as the chief justice in the land ushered in the revised copyright extension. Eldred was represented by Stanford law professor Lawrence Lessig, who was supported more widely by a range of pressure groups, university law professors and even large IT corporations including Intel. Lessig's basic argument in suing the US government was that extending the length of the author's basic reproduction right from life plus fifty years to life plus seventy years represented a hindrance to creativity by limiting the knowledge and information available in the public domain. Put more precisely, Lessig argued that 'We want the right to copy verbatim works that should be in the public domain and would be in the public domain but for a statute that cannot be justified under ordinary First Amendment analysis or under a proper reading of the limits built into the Copyright Clause' (*Eldred v Ashcroft*, No. 01-618).

Eldred had raised the issue initially because some of the literature available on his site had been brought back under copyright due to the 1998 Act. The Act also represented the eleventh such extension to copyright in a period of forty years. Ultimately, the Act was seen as another instance of Congress changing the law to suit the interests of multinational corporations over the wider public interest. What has driven the lengthening of the copyright term, not only in the USA but in legislation around the world, is the opening up of new media markets ripe for the exploitation of old and existing media content in new and innovative ways. However, rather than opening up copyright regimes to enable innovative uses of new media forms such as the Internet, legislators are of one mind that the only way to encourage the expansion of the media industries is through the incorporation of new media content into the existing copyright regimes. As the *Eldred v Ashcroft* case exemplified, in actuality the legislature has extended copyright into unprecedented terrain, recapturing content previously in the public domain and ultimately reassuring those at the head of giant media corporations like Disney that they will not lose control of some of their prized assets. The other reason for the lengthening of the copyright term has been the process of globalisation. As media markets have expanded, so too has their protection under intellectual-property law.

Internationalisation of copyright?

There is no such thing as a homogenised international copyright, and individual nation states have their own histories of copyright legislation. In spite of increasing co-operation between trading nations of the world, the levels of protection, and particular areas of emphasis regarding the status of the author of original works, also differ around the world. This has produced confusion and conflict in the international trade of copyrighted material, as inconsistencies in the scale of protection afforded in various nations of the world remain. This is particularly pronounced where copyrighted works are traded or pirated across national borders. For example, the importation of a work without the consent of the owner, or where the owner's consent is given to manufacture the work exclusively outside the UK, would directly infringe copyright in the UK. Attempts to rectify the disparities and divergences of copyright regimes around the world have given rise to a range of international agreements in order to harmonise minimum standards of protection and enforcement. Some of these multilateral agreements operate as broad guidelines in which nations can develop copyright law. The Berne Convention, first signed by 100 nations in 1886, constituted a union under which a system of reciprocal protection of copyrighted works could be developed. The Berne Convention came in part as a response to a period of concerted pressure from a group of authors, led by the French romantic author Victor Hugo, who were perturbed by a rising tide of pirated books as the mass publication of books became more feasible from the mid-nineteenth century. The Convention has been amended several times as media technologies have evolved and new rights have emerged. As the Convention makes clear, its aim is to guarantee the rights of the author within the union and signatory nations:

> Authors shall enjoy, in respect of works for which they are protected under this Convention, in countries of the Union other than the country of origin, the rights which their respective laws do now or may hereafter grant to their nationals, as well as the rights specially granted by this Convention. (Article 5(1), The Berne Convention)

The Convention is administered by the World Intellectual Property Organisation (WIPO), which was founded under the auspices of the United Nations in 1967. However, in spite of being in existence for more than a century, the Berne Convention, and others like it such as the Universal Copyright Convention agreed under the auspices of UNESCO in 1952, have arguably failed to bring any adequate, substantive level of harmonisation to copyright around the world.

TRIPS and its discontents

Far more potent in its authority and reach has been the Agreement on Trade-Related Intellectual Property Rights, otherwise known as TRIPS. TRIPS was formed under the Final Act (1994) of the Uruguay Round of GATT negotiations that began in 1986 when government ministers from around the world met to negotiate the terms of international trade of what would eventually become the World Trade Organisation. High on the agenda of TRIPS was the move to establish multilateral agreements that set minimum levels of protection available for intellectual property rights across global markets. The agreement established four basic principles:

1. minimum substantive standards of protection of intellectual property rights;
2. the prescription of procedures and remedies which should be available in member states to enforce rights;
3. making available the general dispute-settlement mechanism of the WTO to address TRIPs-related conflicts;
4. the extension of basic GATT principles such as transparency and non-discrimination with trading partners to the provision of intellectual property rights.

The TRIPs Agreement builds on the treaties overseen by the WIPO, with additional international rules governing rental rights to authors of computer software, protection to producers of sound recordings from the unauthorised recording and broadcasting of live performances (otherwise known as 'bootlegging'), the minimum length of protection for sound recordings and performers to be at least fifty years; and the granting of a minimum twenty years' protection for the authorisation to use previously broadcast programmes. TRIPS was the first global standard on intellectual property rights that treated trademarks, copyright and patents as key tools of international trade, not just a mechanism for rewarding innovation and creativity. Moreover, the Treaty was not only viewed as a key mechanism for global trade in intellectual property-related products but crucially a motivating force for developing nations to access lucrative export markets in the industrial world, particularly in areas of information technology that also had strong links to the media and entertainment industries.

WTO members are obliged to provide effective enforcement procedures and remedies for intellectual property-rights holders (i.e. injunctions, damages or criminal proceedings) as well as measures to be taken by border customs authorities when counterfeit or pirated goods are confronted (i.e. by seizure). The approach taken in the TRIPS Agreement is akin to the implementation of an EU Directive: it specifies certain objectives (minimum standards), but leaves its signatories to determine how these requirements are implemented. Where WIPO operates as a secretariat of global intellectual property conventions, the WTO carries powerful political and economic remedies and sanctions over nations that fail to meet the minimum standards of TRIPS. This has significant implications for developing nations, struggling to enter the global marketplace, that have had to adopt intellectual property regimes originating in advanced capitalist nations such as Britain and the United States.

It is because of the application of Western principles of private property to the rest of the world that TRIPS has raised a number of highly contentious issues among developing nations, not least over the stripping away of indigenous knowledge and resources by transnational corporations only interested in enforcing intellectual property for commercial gain. Shiva (2001), Correa (2000) and Drahos and Braithwaite (2002) have all pointed out the imbalance of power and influence enshrined in TRIPS that massively favours the United States and the European Community over other trading regions of the world. As Shiva (2001) has noted, the control of intellectual property rights under TRIPS is tacitly one-sided in favour of corporate rights at the expense of basic human and community rights in developing nations. She notes in respect of patents: 'The pressure to have a globally enforceable uniform patent system is not justified on the basis of empirical evidence of the impact of patents on the public good, especially in the Third World' (Shiva, 2001: 8).

Critiques of TRIPS are understandable when people's health or livelihoods are threatened by corporate interests and control of intellectual property rights concerning life-saving drugs or basic agricultural resources such as seeds and fertiliser. However, in the context of the media and entertainment industries, the economic and cultural costs of TRIPS are masked by long-standing practices of the media industry and the structures of power and influence that have evolved through the twentieth century.

A critique becomes a little clearer when we consider the kind of markets that TRIPS and other global treaties of its kind attempt to control.

The rise of the global economy has been heavily equated with the move from industrial to knowledge-based economies. As sociologists such as Manuel Castells (2000) have pointed out, developed Western economies of North America and Europe are viewed as dominated by service industries whose currency is knowledge. Protecting and exploiting knowledge therefore becomes a key tool in building new markets both domestically and internationally. Again, if we look at the United States, throughout the bulk of the twentieth century it was a net importer of copyrighted products. However, in the final two decades of the century, the USA became a net exporter of copyrighted content from television programmes and films to software licences and computer games (Howkins, 2001). In such a context, it is no surprise that the USA has wanted to extend the reach of copyright as far and as deeply as possible into the various national markets of the world. Changes in the globalisation of media content and the need to ensure reciprocity for US copyright holders in foreign markets eventually led to the USA joining the Berne Convention in 1989. The USA had previously been reluctant to join the international union because of the inclusion of moral rights that gave authors and composers control over the way in which their work is presented or manipulated. The trade-off of membership, however, has been an institutional basis from which to fight piracy and introduce US copyright principles to other members. As we shall discover in the next chapter, the US media industries have been relatively successful on both counts through litigation against mounting piracy and as leading advocates of new WIPO treaties that attempt to control media content in the digital environment.

One significant consequence of this process has been an increase in 'the flows of capital and technology to developing countries' (Correa, 2000: 23) from the developed world to Third World nations. The rhetoric of creating a level playing field in the international trade of copyrighted works is therefore nothing less than a fallacy. According to Drahos and Braithwaite (2002), the globalisation of trade laws in intellectual property has established what they call 'infogolopolies' dominated by the needs of large multinational media corporations to maintain their dominance in global markets. They point out that this process has been occurring since the turn of the twentieth century, epitomised by the cartels established in the US film industry which were premised on 'patents over film and the manufacture of projectors' that effectively 'knitted cartel members together' (Drahos and Braithwaite, 2002: 175). Hollywood's dominance of the worldwide film industry emerged from the vertical control of production, distribution and exhibition assisted by US trade commissioners and backed by the threat of unilateral trade sanctions by the US government where nations failed to play by their rules. Drahos and Braithwaite emphasise the potential damage which the Hollywood system of global cultural production can cause to other national production systems. Hollywood's grip on the film and television industries protected under the wing of globally harmonised intellectual property rights enables the exploitation of particular media assets – from Mickey Mouse to *The Matrix* – in multiple ways in many different markets. As the authors point out, this hegemony is not rooted in the dominance of one centralised location of media power: 'Hollywood these days does not represent so much a place as a distinctive business approach to cultural production which makes entertainment its loadstar' (Drahos and Braithwaite, 2002: 178). As we shall discover in Part Two of this book, the ways and means by which the USA dominates various sectors of the media industry in terms of market structure and corporate practices is overwhelming.

Parallel imports of media products

The legislation is not altogether clear, however, regarding the 'parallel importation' of material (known as 'grey goods'). Parallel importation occurs when copyright material is imported to an indigenous market from elsewhere, even though the product may already exist in that territory. The reasons for parallel imports are usually availability (that is, stocks of a work may exist outside one market but be prevalent in another) or cost (works may be cheaper in other territories due to economic circumstances or discriminative pricing by the manufacturer or distributor). In most cases, importation will not have been sanctioned by the copyright holder. Why can this happen? Once a copyright owner's exclusive right to issue copies to the public has been given, the owner cannot prevent their resale. This is known as the first sale doctrine, and the original distributor's rights are said to be exhausted. However, this only concerns the right of distribution of the goods. Therefore, the economic value of performance works, such as a film, lies in the copyright owner's ability to continue authorising its performance. In the case of a film, this would be by its repeated broadcast to different national audiences. Here, copyright's power to authorise performance is not exhausted even when the distribution right has been.

Media companies have been keen to prevent parallel importation as much as possible, as it has the potential to undermine territorial markets. The flooding of cheap DVDs from South-East Asia to the UK, for example, would be viewed by many in the industry as seriously undermining the market in the UK for the same content. However, if it was clear to the consumer that the imported DVD did originate in another country, it may well be deemed acceptable, for the imported DVDs would not be passed off to deceive the consumer that they were the same as copyright DVDs in the UK. The practice of importing CDs, particularly from the USA and Japan, has been common practice among some music retailers and can be used as a means of accessing rare and alternative versions of albums released in the UK. In spite of these practices, challenges are still being mounted by copyright holders over the legitimate jurisdictions for parallel importation to take place. At present, members of the EU operate a regional policy on parallel importation that accepts that goods bought within one member state are then said to be exhausted across the EEA.

Instances of music companies threatening sanctions on music retailers for practising parallel importation have not been uncommon. In Australia, Sony Music Entertainment made threats to withdraw certain retail privileges from certain outlets because they were stocking parallel imports, in some instances threatening to cut off the supply of certain albums altogether. The Australian Competition and Consumer Commission (ACCC) investigated Sony's threats and concluded that the music company and its distribution company had severely restricted trade and had abused their market power in trying to protect territorial copyright. The ACCC also heard cases involving similar breaches of power by Warner Music Group and Universal Music Group (ACCC, 2001).

Given the increasing harmonisation of global trade and its regulation, there is a strong argument for exhaustion to apply on an international scale, enabling consumers to find the goods they desire via the cheapest distributional outlets. In the era of Internet-based distribution and sales, in particular through sites such as e-Bay, it is increasingly difficult to argue a case against parallel imports.

The harmonisation of copyright in the European Union

The European Union's approach to intellectual property, and to copyright in particular, is in line with its broader commitment to a single European market and general harmonisation of statutes within member states. The issue of copyright has gradually taken centre stage within the EU's regulations on the media industry and internal market, especially regarding its vision of producing a coherent response to the information society. The EU identifies particular issues which are of general importance for the application of copyright to digital technologies. Since 1987, the EU has introduced no fewer than eight directives relating to intellectual property, with a ninth on the enforcement of intellectual property progressing to completion in 2004. The thrust of most of these directives has been to adapt intellectual property protection to new digital technologies. As we shall discuss in more detail in Chapter 3, there are some wide-ranging issues raised by digital media for the ownership, control and protection of media rights. However, following on from our concern with the media industries' drive to persuade legislators to harmonise intellectual property regimes across territorial borders, we shall now look briefly at recent developments at the European level.

Digitalisation, new market structures and cross-border services raise a number of specific legal issues, not least the identification of the 'author', the application of the traditional concept of 'originality' as the premise for protection, the concept of 'fair use' and other exceptions, and the general scope of exclusive rights in reproduction, performance and distribution.

The EC Directive (2001/29/EC) on the harmonisation of certain aspects of copyright and related rights in the information society requires legislative action by member states with respect to four areas: (1) the reproduction right; (2) the communication to the public right; (3) the distribution right; and (4) protection against the circumvention or abuse of electronic management and protection systems. The Directive offers an extensive range of associated rights relating to the information society which mirror EU members' signed agreement to the WIPO Copyright Treaty (1996) and the WIPO Performances and Phonograms Treaty (1996). The Directive was transposed into national copyright law and in the UK became an amendment to the 1988 Act as the Copyright and Related Rights Regulations (2003).

The EC's position matches the general movement to assert copyright protection, but it did not find an easy ride into the European legislature. The Directive was one of the most embattled ever passed by the EU, and took more than four years to be adopted. The Directive does not introduce radical changes to the existing regulatory regime on copyright; instead, it recognises that it is the media environment that is undergoing extraordinary change, to which the basic tenets of copyright law and concepts can be applied. But there are important changes to the definition of what constitutes a copyright work, and the Directive introduces brand new laws to protect certain technological aspects of copyright protection. We shall discuss some of the broader issues of anti-circumvention laws in the next chapter, specifically relating to similar legislation in the USA where the adoption of the WIPO treaties has led to controversial court battles regarding ownership of rights and fair use. However, it is important to point out in this brief review of European action towards the internationalisation of copyright protection that the EU has gone to extreme lengths to ensure that all members are beginning to sing from the same song sheet.

The regulations governing the technological measures to protect media rights have come under close scrutiny, and the 2001 Copyright Directive was designed to bring about a degree of harmony in national legislation to ensure reciprocity across the Union. In the context of intellectual property law and the varied philosophical traditions that underlie legislation in member states, the attempt to harmonise copyright has proved difficult. For example, the Directive gives member states several exemptions to Article 6 that sets out the anti-circumvention rules, which also gives room for varied interpretation of what 'anti-circumvention' means and what exceptions might be enacted. The exceptions centre around fair use for copying works in libraries and museums, for educational uses, for purposes of parody and for criticism or review. All of these activities might be interpreted differently because they are reliant to a certain degree on the cultural meaning and understanding of such practices. The variance in the application of the Directive may therefore render some acts in the EU as infringement in one nation but within the law in another. For instance, exemptions to allow the circumvention of copyright protection measures for scientific research have been deemed acceptable in Germany but not in the UK. Different interpretations of the Directive are further exacerbated by the incremental implementation of the Copyright Directive across EU nations. By July 2002, fewer than half of the member states had introduced new legislation transposing the Directive. The initial deadline for implementation was December 2002. For the ten new member states of the EU who joined in May 2004, the process of implementing the Copyright Directive is likely to take even longer given their historical paucity of intellectual property-rights regimes and the need to debate their way around the various exceptions available.

Conclusion

Certain copyright lobbies, particularly from the software manufacturers who have been hit by 'piracy rates' calculated at 36 per cent across Europe in 2003 by the Business Software Alliance (Geitner, 2004), have emphasised the need for absolute harmonisation of rights and stricter policing of copyright infringement across EU states and indeed around the world. However, different cultural practices and different historical intellectual property regimes mean that there shall always be subtle differences in the application of copyright laws, with different emphasis placed on either rights pertaining to authors (for example, the strong moral rights enjoyed under the French Intellectual Property Code) or exceptions for fair use supported by scientific or education use. Nevertheless, pressure from global media corporations and their trade associations such as the Motion Picture Association of America (MPAA), the International Federation of Phonogrammes Industries (IFPI) and the Business Software Alliance (BSA) already mentioned, has certainly not fallen on deaf ears and has persuaded both the EU nations to implement a series of key copyright and rights-related statutes to protect and enhance their economic interests. The balancing act of copyright, laid out in the earlier part of this chapter, does appear to be at risk. Indeed, some might argue that users' and consumers' rights in the copyright deal have already been superseded by the demands of the media industries to maintain control of their 'assets'. As we shall move on to discuss in the next chapter, the introduction of technological measures to police copyright has inflamed fierce criticism from some consumer groups and advocates of information freedom. Similarly, authors and creators of cultural works have ironically seen some of their rights undermined by the commercial principles that now drive copyright protection. As we shall discover when we look at different sectors of the media industries later in the book, the utilitarian, market-driven principles of copyright as they are interpreted by contemporary global media companies have increasingly become the *de facto* understanding of how media rights are organised and distributed. But, before we look at individual market circumstances for various media industries, we shall first review the problems which digital media pose for copyright and how legislators and the media industries have attempted to cope with this threat.

Study question

A discussion point for this chapter centres on the question of whether copyright facilitates creativity in the media industry or whether it presents a barrier to expression of original ideas. This is a theme we shall revisit in Chapter 9, but it is at the heart of many philosophical and political debates about intellectual property in general.

Further reading

Cornish, W. R. and D. Llewelyn (eds) (2003), *Intellectual Property: Patents, Copyrights, Trademarks and Allied Rights*, London: Sweet and Maxwell.
Hart, T. and L. Fazzani (2003), *Intellectual Property Law*, 2nd edn, London: Palgrave-Macmillan.
Lutzker, A. P. (2003), *Content Rights for Creative Professionals: Copyrights and Trademarks in a Digital Age*, 2nd edn, Burlington: Focal Press.

Relevant websites

TRIPS – http://www.wto.org/english/tratop_e/trips_e/trips_e.htm

The Berne Convention – http://www.wipo.int/treaties/en/ip/berne/index.html

UK Patent Office – http://www.patent.gov.uk/

UK Intellectual Property – http://www.intellectual-property.gov.uk/

Copyright Licensing Authority – http://www.cla.co.uk/

IP Europe – http://www.ip-europe.org/

3 Copyright in the digital age

Thomas Jefferson advanced the concept of libraries and the right to check out a book free of charge. But this great forefather never considered the likelihood that 20 million people might access a digital library electronically and withdraw its contents at no cost.

(Nicholas Negroponte, *Being Digital*, 1996: 4)

Digital technology could enable an extraordinary range of ordinary people to become part of a creative process. To move from the life of a 'consumer' (just think about what that word means – passive, couch potato, fed) of music – and not just music, but film, and art, and commerce – to a life where one can individually and collectively participate in making something new.

(Lawrence Lessig, *The Future of Ideas*, 2001: 9)

Introduction

The balancing act that copyright attempts to achieve between the author of a work and the circulation of information and cultural knowledge that we analysed in the previous chapter has come under increasing attack. As the citation above by Lawrence Lessig suggests, the turn in what some have called the 'digital moment' (Vaidhyanathan, 2001) and others have interpreted as the 'digital dilemma' (National Research Council, 2000) has collapsed the distinctions between media producers and media consumers. While the use and reuse of media in cultural creativity is not necessarily a new thing, from jazz to hip-hop, it is the ability of more and more people to create and disseminate their creative output which is new and potentially radical.

Digitalisation, the movement of information by means of binary digits or 'bits', has meant that all forms of media can be easily manipulated, thereby undermining the ways in which copyright works both to promote creativity and to control copying. Digital media has the potential to collapse many of the distinctions that analogue media upheld and around

31

which copyright has historically been formulated. For example, the ease with which consumers of media products can rapidly become producers of media through desktop publishing, music and video editing, digital photography and web design radically subverts any basic distinctions we might hold between the author, producer, distributor and the audience. This chapter sets out to analyse why digital media have such far-reaching consequences for media rights and how governments and media industries have attempted to maintain regulation of the digital environment through new legislation and technological means. But first we shall look at exactly why digital media pose a threat.

Digital lives

There can be little doubt that digital media have opened our eyes to the potential panoply of creative ideas that are now available to us. The computer on which I wrote this book has capabilities far beyond the assemblage of simple text. I can link up a digital video camera and import clips into my video-editing software. These can be cropped and edited, transformed and reordered with fancy title sequences to create a home-made movie all of my own making. I can then add an accompanying soundtrack and 'burn' the movie on to a DVD to share with my friends and family. A few years ago, the capability of producing such a multimedia product was beyond my technical capacity and ken. But now, as the Apple advertisement proclaimed when they introduced their multicoloured range of iMacs, I can 'rip, mix and burn' along with the rest of the digital authors filling the everyday cultural spaces of our lives. Such DIY digital media seem fine; but what if I attempted to use this technology to edit existing movies produced by a film company I had bought on DVD? What issues would arise? To answer these questions, let's look at another hypothetical snapshot of our digital lives.

In the context of copyright, the first question to be faced would be whether or not after purchasing a commercial DVD I had any right to make a copy. Under copyright law, once I have bought a DVD, any rights in the disk are said to be exhausted. That is, technically I am able to do as I wish with the disk, as it is mine. Or is it? I may be able to lend the DVD to a friend or even resell it via e-Bay, but what I do not have permission to do (so it tells me on the DVD cover sleeve) is strip out the content of the DVD and reproduce it on my computer. The practice of copying media once we have bought it is now such a part of everyday life that people do it without thinking twice about copyright. Digital media and computers make the job of reproducing media even simpler. However, DVDs, the fastest-growing new media technology *ever*, prevent us from conducting this seemingly innocuous act, something we have done for years with our music collections. One reason why the film industry does not want us to make copies of DVDs is that they are near-perfect reproductions. One characteristic of digital media is the ability to make copies without any degradation to the quality of the work. If multiple near-perfect copies of DVDs could legitimately be made, the exclusive market for licensed distributors of DVDs could potentially be undermined by a flood of cheap imitations that look as good as the original.

The issue of perfect reproduction leads us to a second related issue concerning the ability of computer users to copy DVDs on to their hard drives. When the motion-picture industry introduced the DVD format, they did so in the knowledge that a media technology that could potentially be copied *ad infinitum* without degradation in the quality of sound and image could harm their market. Therefore they introduced some technological barriers to complement the legislative measures already in place to prevent copying under copyright. This is chiefly because media corporations do not trust the consumer not to breach copyright law. So, if we return to the analogy of trying to copy a DVD to my Apple iMac, I would find that it would not be technologically possible with the software provided. Why? Because DVDs come with important access controls. The content-scrambling system (CSS) is an encryption system that makes it difficult for a user to play a DVD unless it is through a licensed machine. In addition, although my Mac is licensed to play DVDs under the CSS licence, it does not enable me to copy or import the digital information embedded in the DVD on to my hard disk. This technological innovation is built into the DVD system and is specifically designed to disable any potential reproduction of DVD content and nip in the bud digital film piracy. As Lessig points out, 'Try to "rip, mix, [and] burn" Disney's *102 Dalmatians* and it's your computer that will get ripped, not the content' (Lessig, 2001: 11). Lessig notes that it is increasingly the code in the software that protects digital media content like DVDs, and the machines they play on also protect these codes.

Digital rights management (DRM)

Transformations in the ability to reproduce, distribute and publish information are increasingly allied to new ways of controlling media rights and how they are managed. As we have already discovered, the information society has produced a range of challenges to copyright laws, not least the ability of individuals to access and copy large amounts of digital information. The challenge to rights holders is to identify ways in which copyright can be protected without diminishing the wider cultural values of openness, public access and choice that digital media have promised.

Exploring and exploiting the value of digital assets has become a booming industry. Harris (1998: 15) suggests that a 'digital asset is anything of value that (1) exists in digital form, (2) is generated by digital means, or (3) may have value if adapted to digital form'. All manner of materials have been transformed into digital signals, and the process of archiving 'digital property', as Harris calls it, has become an important dimension of media organisations.

The process of digitalisation itself can be formalised in various ways, from the multipurposing of media assets (manipulating information to suit various needs) to the reuse or re-expression of media across various formats. For instance, a news bulletin can be simultaneously posted on the web and sent via e-mail or to mobile phones. Media can also be repurposed, whereby an old tune can be transformed into the latest ringtone.

One of the priorities of media-rights holders has been to introduce digital rights-management (DRM) systems. Encryption and rights-management software have become central to the commercialisation of digital media, especially the boom in e-commerce and interactive television (iTV). Open any broadsheet newspaper or trade journal and you will be sure to find a stylish piece of advertising for a software company offering the latest 'digital solutions'. These technologies not only protect investment in the creation of digital assets by individuals and organisations, they also ensure that content is in a form that is reusable. In other words, they provide more bang for your buck.

DRM systems, such as digital watermarks that scramble data, or data metering that registers use, present technical avenues for preventing illegal appropriation of copyright works. Similarly, digital hardware may be manufactured with measures in mind to prevent illegal copying. We have already mentioned the DRM introduced by the film industry to protect DVDs; but this type of technology is increasingly prevalent across all digital media from copy-protected CDs to the scrambling devices of digital television. Why, we might ask, is the media industry so paranoid?

One story that is instructive in answering this question actually involves a covert struggle between two media giants and the battle to control the booming market for digital television around the world. It is a tale of hackers, espionage and dodgy street-market traders.

In autumn 1998, digital television was introduced for the first time in the UK. First, BSkyB launched their digital platform, shortly followed by new entrant OnDigital, a joint venture by the two major ITV companies Granada and Carlton Communications. In spite of BSkyB's head start in the world of multichannel television, OnDigital, later rebranded ITV

Digital, was bullish about its ability to gain a foothold in the UK pay-TV market. Central to this plan was new technology that enabled subscribers to receive digital broadcasts via a conventional aerial with the encrypted signal descrambled by a set-top-box (STB) decoder. Unfortunately, after only four years, ITV Digital had gone into receivership and eventual liquidation, enabling BSkyB to gain a near-monopoly on the future of digital pay-TV.

One of the reasons why ITV Digital failed was the level of 'piracy' of STB 'smart cards' that decoded the encrypted digital signal. The long-standing fears of the media industry in the digital age were realised when large numbers of viewers were able to circumvent the gateway to subscription TV channels. Encrypted signals that enable access to subscription and pay-per-view content are the bedrock of leveraging revenue from digital multichannel television. Take away the security of encryption and the whole business model is effectively undermined. From the outset, ITV Digital faced a massive problem of counterfeit cards. Estimates ranged from 100,000 to 200,000 pirated cards in circulation at any one time (*The Guardian*, 13 March 2002). Consumers would receive their STB from ITV Digital, subscribe to the minimum subscription service of £6.99 a month and replace their issued smart card by one enabling access to all the premium channels. Pirated cards were distributed via age-old black-market networks in pubs and street markets, and details of updated encryption codes were posted on a monthly basis on the Internet. News that ITV Digital was facing a huge piracy problem surfaced in March 2002 when its main supplier of smart cards, a subsidiary of Vivendi Universal, Canal Plus Technologies, filed a $1bn lawsuit in the US courts regarding the piracy of their technology by rival manufacturer NDS. NDS was 78 per cent owned by News Corporation and operated out of Israel. The company employed 'reformed hackers' to create the code and frustrate the 'pirates'. By August 2004, NDS had supplied 44 million smart cards to pay-TV companies around the world (Milmo, 2004).

Canal Plus claimed that NDS had used their 'reformed hackers' to break their encryption code by reverse-engineering the smart cards. The details were circulated to counterfeiters worldwide via the Internet and criminal networks. This enabled card pirates to recode cards to provide access to all premium channels without payment. The claim of corporate espionage was refuted heavily by NDS and their owners News Corporation. But the levels of piracy of ITV Digital STBs was enormous and seriously damaging to the levels of new subscribers to the flagship ITV Sport channel.

Unfortunately for ITV Digital, the legal action taken by Canal Plus was too late in the day to save the digital platform. The litigation against

NDS was eventually dropped in appeasement a year later after News Corporation had acquired a controlling share of Italian pay-TV platform Telepui from debt-laden Vivendi Universal. Within the space of twelve months, the Sky Global brand had bolstered its position as the leading pay-TV provider across Europe, safe in the knowledge that its technology had not yet been pirated. However, other lawsuits followed in the USA when a host of digital satellite companies including Direct TV (USA), Sogecable (Spain) and Echostar (USA) also brought action against NDS. Again, acquisition of the Direct TV network by News Corporation soon quelled the row, although claims that NDS 'hackers' had undermined digital television networks around the world continued to be heard well into 2004. In defence of these claims, the head of NDS, Abe Peled, argued that it was jealousy driving such accusations. However, ironically, in an interview with the *Guardian* media business correspondent Dan Milmo, he confessed that 'The more money pirates make, the more powerful they are. They will not make money from cracking our platforms, but if they crack other platforms they will make a lot of money. If you make a card for $5 and sell it for $200, it has a better margin than selling drugs' (Milmo, 2004). Surely an incentive for a competitor to leak such information into the public domain?

We can see therefore that DRM software builds and stores the value of media content (much like a virtual bank of digital assets) and acts more or less like a digital lock. DRM can automate the flow of content from one project to the next, can prevent 'undesirables' (or simply those who have not paid) from looking at content, and can even place limitations on the use of a media product after it has been purchased. Clearly, the more content a media organisation owns, the greater its opportunities to re-express information in new ways and contexts. Ironically, the opening up of information in digital networks has given more power to the interests of large media corporations, whose potential 'bank' of digital assets is enormous. Think, for example, of the 1,001 ways in which the return of *Star Wars* in 1999 was used to sell merchandise in digital formats: websites, CDs, DVDs, CD-ROM, video games and so on.

The opportunities to build monopolies in the delivery of information are, therefore, of concern to those who prophesy the democratic principles of the 'information society'. Deregulation of telecommunications and broadcasting has moved to negate the impact of information monopolies; but, ironically, corporate copyright holders are stubbornly attempting to maintain their market positions and exploit their concentration of media rights in the increasingly global marketplace. Where material media products are public at the point of sale (the exhaustion of rights), irrevocable and fixed, digital media tend to have restricted access, with multiple versions and a fleeting existence.

The rise of encrypted media, protected by code, has thrown up a host of contentious issues in an age when digital media promises so much to the user. Encryption and other methods of DRM are posing new issues as to what copyright is for. For many advocates of the empowering nature of digital media, the balance between producers (the corporate media) and users (the consumer, who may also be a potential producer) has been heavily tipped in favour of the former. As we shall go on to discuss further below, how this argument is framed and who is set to benefit deeply affects the way in which copyright law has been expanded in the digital age.

Protecting the digital locks: the WIPO Treaty, the DMCA and the Copyright Directive

The WIPO Copyright Treaty was adopted after the Diplomatic Conference on Certain Copyright and Neighbouring Rights Questions held by WTO members in Geneva in 1996. The conference and subsequent treaty were established in response to the increasing worldwide use of the Internet, and among other things attempted to introduce measures to prevent the importation, distribution or manufacture of protection-defeating technologies.

The Clinton administration was one of the first governments to react to the issues raised by digital media. New legislation emerged from a wholesale review of copyright and the Internet in a white paper entitled Intellectual Property and the National Information Infrastructure (NII), published in 1995. The policy document analysed the potential impact of digital networks on copyright law and was strongly backed by the media and entertainment industries. Critics of the white paper and its architect, Senator Bruce Lehman, were fearful of a 'maximalist agenda' in the protection of copyright ownership and its threat to citizenship on the web (Samualson, 1996). However, the 'maximalist agenda' of the Clinton administration and the 'copyright industries' moved forward to incorporate the WIPO treaties in order to shore up US copyright and its international borders. The US government's response was the Digital Millennium Copyright Act 1998 (DMCA). Although the Act is specifically designed to increase the protection of copyright works on the Internet, it takes a minimalist stance in adhering to the WIPO treaties, in the belief that existing legislation in the USA can deal adequately with the new problems arising from digital media and communications.

The provisions of the new law mainly concentrate on preventing the illegal circumvention of technologies which are aimed at blocking access to copyrighted works. Anti-circumvention provisions were a direct response to Article 11 and Article 12 of the WIPO Copyright Treaty. Article 11 introduced instruments to enable copyright owners to 'challenge the manufacture and sale of technologies or services capable of circumventing technological protection of copyright works', while Article 12 protected the 'integrity of rights-management information attached to protected works in digital form' (Samualson, 1997: 3). Both articles were heavily influenced by the requests of the US media industries (Samualson, 1997) and not surprisingly formed the backbone of the DMCA's adoption of the WIPO provisions. As Fallenbock (2002) reveals, the DMCA anti-circumvention provisions introduced a key distinction between access-circumvention and copy-circumvention. The latter provisions are applicable within copyright law and deal with issues specific to copyright. Therefore, the limitations on fair use that apply to copyright law must also apply to the copy-anti-circumvention provision. However, copyright law does not have any bearing on access provisions, therefore access-anti-circumvention provisions under the DMCA are potentially limitless in their jurisdiction (Fallenbock, 2002: 18).

This 'copyright grab' (Samualson, 1996), as it became known, was viewed as stripping the public of access to information and, most importantly, of undermining the 'fair use' doctrine of private appropriation of copyrighted works. Legitimate uses of works that were protected with DRM technologies became heavily restricted, thereby compromising the balance of copyright law. Driven by the corporate interests of the media industry, anti-circumvention provisions ensured that the digital locks put in place by copyright holders not only acted as a prohibitive mechanism to personal copying but further ensured that anyone who managed to get around such protection was immediately criminalised. As Litman (2001: 143) has observed with regard to the commonplace practice of sharing information electronically,

> Borrowing your brother's password so that you can read a publication he subscribes to but you don't is now illegal. So is using a widely distributed software utility that would permit you to view a DVD movie you purchased on a player manufactured and sold in a different region of the world and licensed to play only DVDs from that region.

The potential lockout from the access and use of copyright works is increasingly extensive and punitive. As Boyle (2003) has argued, it is like a digital 'enclosure movement', where private interests capture and incorporate more and more assets from public culture. This 'enclosure of the intangible commons of the mind' has become more pronounced and all-encompassing, whereby 'things that were formerly thought of as either common property or uncommodifiable are being covered with new, or newly extended, property rights' (Boyle, 2003: 38). The DMCA and the

European Copyright Directive that followed it, and was clearly heavily influenced by its anti-circumvention provisions, was one particular end point of a gradual erosion of the public domain and the commons – the cultural pool of information which we can all draw from and work upon to create and innovate new ideas and new creations. According to Boyle, this process has largely gone unseen at the fringes of intellectual property; but, now that digital locks are increasingly prevalent in the media industries and elsewhere, the public at large is being awoken to the fact that such restrictive laws and technologies actually have an impact on our everyday lives. Boyle's adoption of the environmentalist doctrine, of a rallying call to pull together broad concerns over all manner of encroachments into our cultural rights, also reminds us that we are talking about intangible property and that it is the laws that govern it which affect our access and use of it.

We shall return to this theme in the concluding chapter of the book; but first it is again worthwhile to turn to a specific case study to illustrate the point about anti-circumvention laws within copyright legislation and what it actually means in practice. When the DMCA took effect, one of the first issues that came to the fore was the circumvention of the copy protection incorporated into digital versatile discs (DVDs) introduced by the motion-picture industry to prevent piracy. As we shall now see, this has far-reaching and potentially damaging consequences for the fair use of copyright materials.

DVDs and DeCSS

A DVD is a thin disc five inches in diameter which can store a large amount of digital data. Each DVD can hold the data necessary to display a full-length motion picture and much more besides. Motion pictures stored on DVDs are protected from unauthorised use by means of encryption using a 'content-scrambling system' (CSS). CSS is designed to restrict the playback of an encrypted (scrambled) DVD to a CSS-equipped DVD player or DVD drive, which is capable of decrypting (unscrambling) the DVD. CSS is primarily composed of algorithms and 400 'master keys'. DVDCCA, a trade association of businesses in the movie industry, controls the rights to CSS. DVDCCA licenses the CSS decryption technology to manufacturers of hardware and software for playing DVDs. Each licensee is assigned one or more master keys unique to that licensee. Furthermore, in order to prevent international trade of 'pirated' DVDs, a regionalised system of encryption was established so that, for example, a DVD bought in the USA would not play on a DVD player licensed in Europe. The manufacture of interoperable, deregionalised players has since negated this technological device, but it did nevertheless enable the industry to regionalise the distribution of DVD releases and to operate price discrimination in certain areas to offset the cost of piracy. One outcome of regionalisation was that the DVD format extended the control of the film industry. As Litman (2001: 153) notes, the 'motion-picture industry took the position that since it controlled the content, it was entitled to condition access on any terms it chose'.

In October 1999, a computer program descrambling CSS was posted on the Internet by Jon Johansen, a 15-year-old student from Norway. Johansen had reverse-engineered the CSS on a licensed DVD player to enable him to play a DVD on an unlicensed player, in this case a computer running on the Linux operating system. Although Microsoft and Apple had introduced licensed DVD players in some of their personal computers, Linux, part of the open source movement, had not at this time acquired such a licence for its operating system. DeCSS, as it became known, consisted of computer source code that described a method for playing an encrypted DVD on a non-CSS-equipped DVD player or drive. Soon after its initial publication on the Internet, DeCSS appeared on numerous websites throughout the world. Many other websites provided links to sites that posted information about DeCSS.

On 27 December 1999, DVDCCA initiated an action under the Uniform Trade Secrets Act (UTSA, or 'the Act') against Andrew Bunner, a programmer from California, and numerous other named and un-named individuals who had allegedly republished or 'linked' to DeCSS. DVDCCA alleged that DeCSS 'embodies, uses, and/or is a substantial derivation of [DVDCCA's] confidential proprietary information', and the Californian Attorney General Bill Lockyer called DeCSS a tool for 'breaking, entering and stealing' (Bowman, 2003). DVDCCA had protected this proprietary information by limiting its disclosure to those who had signed licensing agreements prohibiting disclosure to others. DVDCCA alleged that the proprietary information contained in DeCSS had been obtained by wilfully 'hacking' and improperly reverse-engineering CSS software created by the plaintiff's licensee, Xing Technology Corporation (Xing). Xing had allegedly licensed its software to users exclusively under a licence agreement that prohibited reverse-engineering.

Bunner argued that any injunction against his website would violate his First Amendment rights relating to free speech (specifically, technically orientated speech). He also asserted that there was no evidence that he knew or should have known that DeCSS had been created by improper use of any proprietary information. Bunner asked the court to take judicial notice of a Norwegian law that permitted reverse-engineering of computer software for the purpose of achieving 'interoperability' and prohibited any agreement to the contrary. According to Bunner, Johansen had legitimately reverse-engineered Xing's software to create DeCSS so that CSS-encrypted DVDs could be played on computers that run on the Linux operating system. In February 2004, the Californian Court of Appeal concluded that there was no grounds for an injunction against Bunner. It held that, by the time the information had been posted on the Bunner website, the information regarding DeCSS was so widespread that it rendered the CSS trade secret inoperable. The ruling went against a prior decision against a hacker magazine, *2600*, that had also published information on DeCSS. In a case brought by the MPAA alleging the circumvention of the CSS code under the DMCA, the Federal Court ruled that the magazine had fallen foul of the access-anti-circumvention provisions and that in this instance the DMCA was above freedom-of-information rights under the US First Amendment.

Conclusion

Subsequent cases relating to DVDs, most notably a case against 321 Studios, a company distributing software that enabled owners of DVDs to make a personal backup copy for non-commercial purposes, have brought further attention to the problematic nature of anti-circumvention provisions under the DMCA and by association the EC Copyright Directive. 'Fair use' rights have clearly been compromised by the new legislation, which has encroached on previously established cultural practices of accessing and copying legitimately bought media content enjoyed by media consumers for many years.

This is a conundrum for the media industry. Digital media may enable better-quality sound and vision, give greater capacity on which to store information and introduce innovative interactive features, but they also provide a cheaper and potentially near-perfect reproduction facility for consumers, many of whom buy such goods in the belief that once they have acquired a piece of media content they have rights to do with it as they please. One such right is the ability to make private copies of a work. If the copying of vinyl records and cassette tapes has historically been accepted by the music industry and copyright law under fair use, why not the copying of CDs on to recordable CDs? Similarly, if music is allowed to be copied in such ways, why not movies to recordable DVDs? The answer lies in the dual processes of perfect reproduction and instantaneous distribution via the Internet. The industry fears that the ability to reproduce and share digital media with such ease could potentially have dramatic impacts on its business. Moreover, according to the media industry, both processes legitimately shift (or rather narrow) the parameters of fair use.

The industry has attempted to extend its control of digital copyright by technological controls in the guise of DRM. As Suthersanen (2002) observes, in the history of copyright and the introduction of new media technology this effect is not necessarily new. However, the introduction of technological locks, enabling only licensed access to media content, does have some profound consequences for the consumer. Most consumers who acquire new technologies buy into the 'industry standard' of available technology on the market. The DVD format is one of the fastest-growing media technologies of all time. After a slow start, it has enjoyed rapid uptake around the developed world. The reason is the ease of use and significant reduction of the costs of acquiring the technology. However, most consumers are unaware that DVD players are licensed for certain uses and have embedded technology within them that restricts those uses. Furthermore, if the owner of a DVD wanted to make alternative uses of the DVD, such as making a copy on to their computer, they would soon run into specific problems that prohibit such actions. These locks are built into the DVD and will be there in perpetuity. This means that when a copyright work falls out of protection and moves into the public domain – as it ultimately must do – it will be very difficult to appropriate the content from the DVD to make further uses from it. For example, it might be desirable to incorporate material from a DVD into a home movie or multimedia presentation. For those with the know-how, the technology exists to do this, but for most of us we will not get the DRM protecting the content on the DVD, which has very limited uses. This is the tip of a very large iceberg. There is all manner of information and media content that is rapidly being locked away behind DRM technologies. Access is provisional increasingly on a pay-per-use basis. What might once have been open for use in the public domain or the commons has now been enclosed behind digital locks. As we shall discover through the rest of this book, this has consequences for how the media industries are organising their commercial operations and how they are attempting to change their relationships between creators and users of media. We shall return to the wider political issues of digital media and the public domain in the concluding chapter, but in the next five chapters we shall investigate specific aspects of the media industry and how they are coming to terms with these changes in media rights.

Study question

What methods have media companies employed to protect their property in the digital environment? How might technology influence the control and balance of copyright between the media industry and its consumers?

Further reading

Lessig, L. (1999), *Code and Other Laws of Cyberspace*, New York: Basic
Books. In particular Chapter 10.
Litman, J. (2001), *Digital Copyright*, Amherst: Prometheus Books. An
excellent review of the policy environment leading up to the 1998
DMCA.

Relevant websites

WIPO Copyright Treaty – http://www.wipo.int/treaties/en/ip/wct/index
.html
The Digital Millennium Copyright Act 1998 – http://www.copyright
.gov/legislation/dmca.pdf
Anti-DMCA – http://anti-dmca.org/

Part Two

Case studies in media rights

4 Music and copyright

Introduction

The music industry is often overlooked in the analysis of media industries. Indeed, music is often viewed outside the general pantheon of what is meant by 'the media'. Upon close inspection, however, it is clear not only that music is a major media industry in and of itself, but furthermore that it weaves itself into the very fabric of all audio-visual media, and even has a significant presence within print-based media in terms of reviews and promotion. The potential areas in which music can be produced, recorded and performed are far more expansive than any other. For example, just think about where in your everyday life you might expect to hear a piece of music: on the radio or in the car; on television across the whole range of genres or in film; or on a specific occasion, at a concert or nightclub.

In the examples above, music takes a leading role in the core activity of entertainment. A report by the DCMS on the state of the British music industry found that it generates £3.2bn in value to the UK economy and earns £1.3bn through exports (DCMS, 2001). Alternatively, think of where music enters your life in a more indirect way: when you enter a shop, a bar, a cafe, a hotel or even a lift; when you are put on hold on the telephone or hear the call of a mobile phone; or when you enter someone else's home or even the workplace. All of the above are recognised uses of music, some paid for, others not. Some are legitimate and others may not be in the context of copyright. The potential for music rights to be used is far-reaching, and how music is used and how its use is monitored and paid for is at the heart of copyright in the music industry.

In terms of production, music is made in multifarious ways, in locations that span the private domain of people's homes, to the recording studios that support the global corporate music industry. Music may be written (in notation) or in lyrics. It may be performed live or it may be recorded. It may also be stored digitally in a computer, in one or many places simultaneously and in various formats. All forms of music may be subject to copyright on creation, but it is not always so clear who is the originator or 'author' of the work being produced, especially if, as is usually the case, there is more than one contributor to the work. Similarly, in some instances, it is not clear if a piece of music has been produced at all – that is, can all sounds be considered to be music? Alternatively, 'authors' may not realise that they can benefit from a copyrighted work, especially if its use has changed from its original production – as in the case of sampling.

Keeping in mind these multifarious aspects of media production and consumption, we shall now discuss the main elements of music copyright, focusing on its relationship to the economics of the industry and the mechanics of copyright protection within the business.

Origins of music copyright

The contemporary recording industry is said to be in crisis because of the capability for digital music files to be shared across networks without remuneration for the artist or producers of the music. We shall discuss peer-to-peer file-sharing and manoeuvres by the industry to quash copyright infringement and introduce legitimate digital downloading services later in the chapter. But, in order to understand what is at stake and why the very structure of the music industry is considered to be under attack, we first need to know how the industry is structured and how media rights form the basis of its commercial enterprise.

Music copyright in the first instance is found in the written/published expression of the composition. Sheet music, therefore, represents the first fixed form of music copyright. Music copyright predates sound recording and is based on the 'notation' of music fixed in printed form. Notation was introduced to remedy the need to standardise the language of music in order for it to be performed time and again by different performers. The publication of music also enabled a method for measuring the use of a work. The number of song sheets sold gave a rough indication of a work's popularity. Clearly, there were problems with such crude measurement of use, and the sale of sheet music tells us little about how the knowledge of a particular piece of music is passed on and subsequently performed. For instance, in a recent survey by the American Society of Composers, Authors and Publishers (ASCAP), the most commonly performed song of the twentieth century was 'Happy Birthday to You', written by Mildred J. Hills and Patty Hill in 1883. Of the people who perform this song, 99.9 per cent do not need sheet music to do so, and the sales of the song sheet would not tell us anything about such widespread use. Where music copyright in the sheet music is important, and potentially lucrative, is in the licensing of the rights to perform and record the music for commercial use. The publishing rights for 'Happy Birthday to You' are owned by Summy-Birchard Music, a subsidiary of the media conglomerate Time Warner, reported to be earning approximately $2m in royalties each year (snopes.com, 2002).

The right to perform a piece of music has its origins in the café society of Paris, where composers sought remuneration for the public recital of their music. The Société des Auteurs, Compositeurs et Editeurs de Musique (SACEM) was founded in 1850 to protect the rights of composers enraged by unlicensed performances, reflecting the strong French tradition of moral rights that prevented others from illegitimately claiming paternal authorship of a work (Laing, 1993). The British tradition was somewhat different; indeed, the performance of other people's songs in music halls was viewed as being an important promotional tool in the sale of sheet music. The idea of charging for a licence to use the music in public did not gain ground until the twentieth century with the innovation of recorded music. The Berne Convention (1886) had provided protection for authors of literary and artistic works (including music) and was amended to include the protection of authors' rights in 'sound recordings' in 1908. A further amendment in 1928 assigned authors' rights in the sound broadcasting of their works, with a subsequent amendment for television in 1948. The licensing of music soon became the bedrock of the commercial activity of a booming record industry.

Collecting societies

The economics of the music industry is based on a 'basket of rights' that protects works for composers, publishers, performers and producers (record companies). Rights may be assigned (which more or less equates to the outright sale of copyright to a particular piece of music) or licensed. It is this licensed use, the sanction for certain uses of music, that makes up a large part of the commercial transactions within the industry. Given the multiple uses of music and the traffic in music works, from publishers to performers to broadcasters, it would be unmanageable for each rights holder to police each and every use of their work themselves. The task of licensing the use of music copyright has been passed on to a range of collecting societies who oversee the administration of rights on behalf of rights owners. By issuing licences centrally on behalf of rights owners, the use of copyright music can be tracked more readily and also provide a one-stop shop for users of music.

Collecting societies are non-profit agencies which have three main functions:

1. to license works in which they hold copyright for specific uses
2. to monitor use and collect revenues
3. to distribute the revenue as royalties to members on a 'pay-per-use' basis.

The administration of these tasks is a significant undertaking, but has proved the most efficient means to date of spreading the costs of licensing. The main rights and licensing organisations in the UK are:

- The Performing Rights Society (PRS)
- The Mechanical Copyright Protection Society (MCPS)
- Phonographic Performance Limited (PPL)
- Video Performance Limited (VPL)
- The Performing Artists' Media Rights Association (PAMRA).

These societies are responsible for collecting revenues from the various rights associated with the use of music. For composers, songwriters and musicians, the two most important rights in this respect are *performance rights* and *mechanical rights*. The Performing Rights Society collects and distributes royalties on behalf of composers and publishers for the public performance and broadcast of music made by its members. Composers and publishers assign their 'rights in performance' – in public, in broadcast and cable services (including the Internet) – over to the PRS, handing over the ownership of such rights. The PRS licenses performers and broadcasters to use the works within the agreed assignment, and in return collects and distributes a royalty fee.

Recent tracking of performing-rights revenues has highlighted that royalty payments across world markets have risen since the early 1990s as the number of broadcasting licences has grown exponentially with the profusion of new satellite and cable channels. Greater enforcement of public performances in new areas of the leisure industry – for example, fitness centres – has also boosted revenues. The PRS collections reached £283.2m in 2003, £242.5m of which was redistributed to its members (www.prs.co.uk). The importance of blanket licences with major broadcasters is emphasised by the size of the rights collected from broadcasters in 2003 – worth £89.6m.

The society also has the right to claim royalties from overseas under the reciprocal treatment of authors under the Berne Convention and TRIPS, which annually makes up nearly a third of its collections (£92.2m in 2003). However, under pressure from the US National Licensed

Beverage Association throughout the 1990s, the US government introduced the Fairness in Music Licensing Act (1998). The legislation introduced certain categories of exemptions to US business premises (including certain types of bar and restaurant) and has caused a backlash from EU member states on the grounds that the law breaks reciprocal obligations under both the Berne Convention and the TRIPS agreement. The EU calculated that both US and EU copyright owners were losing up to $43 million in royalty payments. In July 2000, the World Trade Organisation upheld the complaint by the EU, recommending that the USA amend its legislation in line with the TRIPS agreement. In spite of the global machinations of the recording industry, disputes of this kind raise our awareness of a certain lack of harmonisation in particular areas of international intellectual-property legislation. One can only understand such discrepancies in the light of the power of the US corporate sector to dominate and manipulate global media markets.

A new addition to the field of performing rights is the payment to performers for the broadcast of their recorded performances, known as *performers' rights* (as distinct from *performance rights*). Receiving royalty payments for recorded performances was introduced under the Copyright and Related Rights Regulations 1996 as a response to the 1992 EC Rental Directive. As Taylor and Towse (1998) outline, the new and extended rights were premised on the 'equitable remuneration' of artists with the producers of sound recordings. Under the 'pay-for-use' doctrine of the EC Directive, the user of sound recordings is responsible for ensuring that payment is given – in this case, an even 50:50 split between artist and record company. However, UK legislation, which puts the onus on copyright owners (or their representatives) to collect fees, hands more power to the record companies because the cost of collection is passed on to the artist. In a battle to rectify this imbalance and to act on behalf of performers, the Performing Artists' Media Rights Association (PAMRA) was founded by the Musicians' Union, Equity, the Incorporated Society of Musicians and Re-Pro. Performers' payments are categorised according to their level of contribution, with featured performers receiving 65 per cent of collected royalties, non-featured performers receiving 35 per cent of collected royalties, and sampled performers receiving a small proportion of non-featured payments. As we shall discuss below, this arbitrary arrangement reflects the industrial practices of the music business, where the value of performances is reduced to an economic value that places power in the hands of company lawyers who negotiate the worth of a recording dependent on its sale in the market.

The introduction of sound recording brought new rights to publishers, composers and songwriters, known as *mechanical rights*. This is the right to record a work which in the contemporary context may include the main 'music carriers' – vinyl, tape, compact discs and DVD – as well as a host of other electronic formats such as minidisks, DAT, MP3 and assorted digital storage devices and platforms associated with new information technologies from computers to mobile phones. The Mechanical Copyright Protection Society (MCPS) represents composers and publishers of music and collects mechanical royalties from sound recordings of copyrighted works from the producers of CDs, records, tapes, videos, film, television, radio and multimedia. Collection of distributable royalties reached £226.9 million in 2003 (www.prs.co.uk), with a high percentage of these revenues coming from blanket licences being signed with major broadcasters. In 1998, the MCPS formed 'The Alliance' with the PRS to centralise the monitoring and collection of royalties of UK-based artists and publishers. In the past, the rights in sound recordings that are assigned to the MCPS were more lucrative than 'performing rights' because the former were calculated on record sales, which had been the most lucrative area of the music industry. However, royalty payments for both performing rights are gradually reaping more rewards as the number of public outlets for music increases (especially with on-line radio). One interesting feature of the royalty-fee structure is that the money recovered is based on a percentage of the published price to the dealer of CDs, records or tapes, which currently operates at around 9 per cent. The volume of sales is based on an audit of 'sound carriers' that have been manufactured. However, pressure is mounting from the record companies to change this calculation because, in the highly competitive market of record sales, companies are undercutting their rivals and will provide dealers with discounts to move large quantities of specific albums or singles. Price competition from UK supermarkets and online retailers such as Amazon has squeezed the margins that record companies previously enjoyed. The claim is that the mechanical royalty fee should be based on a percentage of the 'average realised price' (ARP) of a recording (the amount it actually sells for). This would require an audit of record-company revenues derived from sales. However, mechanical collecting societies around the world have so far refused to transfer systems because the ARP is more costly and time-consuming to monitor.

As well as the rights in publishing music, as either composer or publisher, legislation also recognises rights in a sound recording which become the ownership of the record company or producer. PPL was established in 1934 to look after such *neighbouring rights* in the interests of record companies, in response to the rise in use of sound recordings in radio broadcasts (in the formative years of radio, most music was performed live or prerecorded in broadcasting studios). PPL administers the public performance and broadcasting rights of recordings and licenses a range of venues and broadcasting organisations to use its members' music. As the number of independent radio stations and satellite and cable stations has increased, PPL has seen a rapid rise in its revenues. From 1988 to 2003, the income from sound-recording licences increased from £16.6m to more than £80m (see the PPL website). Payments to performers on behalf of record companies were once based on 'ex gratia' payments (featured performers were given voluntary remuneration). This has changed in the light of the 1992 EC Rental Directive (92/100/EEC) that holds that performers have a statutory right to share in sound-recording revenue. Legislation in the UK has been introduced to require direct payments to featured performers (20 per cent of PPL revenues) and non-featured performers (12 per cent of PPL revenues). However, one issue raised by these changes is whether or not musicians have lost out in other areas of income. As Towse (2004) suggests, breaking down payments in the music industry is riven with difficulties, as many payments are hidden in the general 'basket of rights'. Whether royalty and studio payments have been reduced due to the change in legislation is open to interpretation (Towse, 2004: 66).

The public performance of sound recordings is licensed under a series of tariffs dependent on the wide range of uses they include: shops, clubs, pubs, hotels, leisure facilities and restaurants. Keeping track of these uses is clearly time-consuming and vulnerable to misuse. The use of sound recordings in broadcasting is meticulously monitored by 'usage returns' which broadcasters are obliged to complete. The returns provide information about the recordings used, dates broadcast, record labels, artists, catalogue numbers and the actual playing time. The production of a radio programme, for example, requires detailed timings of each recording used down to the nearest second. Full usage returns are provided by the BBC and twenty-two commercial radio stations. A further ten radio stations are sampled to reflect an estimated figure of use for the remaining stations in the commercial sector. What PPL usage analysis identifies is the challenge of managing rights data in a rapidly expanding digital environment where the number of users is tremendously high. A third mechanism of measurement is the use of music charts as a barometer of usage. The use of these alternative sources, particularly specialist music charts, is very problematical. Some charts are compiled not on the actual volume of sales but on subjective criteria and critical opinion. The position of a track or album in a chart may reflect not sales but more the taste culture of music journalists and editors. Similarly, the tracks that feature most prominently in the broadcast media may not be the most commercially successful in the singles or albums charts. PPL's list of the top twenty most used tracks for 2003 includes Elton John's 'Are you Ready for Love?' that achieved mediocre success in the charts but was heavily used in a promotional campaign by BSkyB in the promotion of its coverage of Premier League football.

The global scale of production and distribution of recordings has led to some emerging alliances between collecting agencies in different countries. In 1999, collecting societies from the USA (ASCAP), the PRS/MCPs Alliance and the Netherlands agency Buma Stemra joined forces to share the handling of music-rights processing in the new digital environment. The objectives of the International Music Joint Venture, as it became known, are to:

1. eliminate duplication in, and improve accuracy of, common databases;
2. reduce costs and improve efficiency;
3. upgrade systems and embrace new technology; and
4. provide an infrastructure to process use in new media.

A similar alliance called 'Fast Track' has also been established by societies from, again, the USA (BMI), France (SACEM), Germany (GEMA), Spain (SGAE) and Italy (SIAE). The idea is to produce an international network using the Internet to create a global virtual database of musical works, including international documentation and distribution, online services for members and customers and the development of an integrated Electronic Copyright Management System.

These strategic moves by the world's largest collection societies are a direct response to the growth in international trade, facilitated by digital networks. They also correspond with similar consolidation among corporate record companies in their production and distribution operations. Several of the largest record companies, including BMG, EMI, Vivendi UMG, Sony and WMG, have developed joint ventures to improve economies of scale due to the cost of shipping CDs and other carriers becoming more onerous. In July 2004, the EC competition authorities sanctioned the merger of Sony and BMG, effectively creating the second largest record company in the world behind Vivendi Universal Music, with the potential to control more than one third of new album sales. Such mega-mergers, seen throughout the global media industries, are reactions to the perceived threat of what they see as music piracy, the rising competition from DVDs and the discounting power of supermarkets that have all impacted on the industry's bottom line. As we shall now discuss, the rhetoric of music piracy runs through the heart of the corporate music world in its strategies to manipulate existing copyright laws and influence new legislation to shore up its dominance and the dominant practices of the music industry.

Music and copyright infringement

The issue of copyright infringement pervades the entire operation and business culture of the music industry. According to the International Federation of Phonographic Industries (IFPI), international piracy costs the recording industry more than $4bn annually. The IFPI also claims that one in three CDs in circulation is pirated. The flow of international piracy is predominantly from the East and the South to the North and the West. In nations where copyright legislation is weak or poorly enforced, pirated copies of music can account for more than 50 per cent of sales in that country (a recent IFPI report on Latvia revealed that 60 per cent of its market in recorded music was counterfeit, with copies flooding in from neighbouring Russia and Ukraine, where large manufacturing plants are based). As we discussed in Chapter 2, music industries have lobbied hard for multilateral agreements to be enforced (i.e. TRIPS) in order to stamp out the illegal duplication, importation, distribution and sale of pirated products.

With the introduction of music on the Internet, the location of information becomes increasingly difficult to trace, especially when digital files are not centralised on a single server. Decentralised software and information makes it virtually impossible to enforce copyright law. In many respects, piracy, either on the Internet or by traditional methods, is viewed as an inevitable part of the music industry. However, it is held by the industry and government that without remuneration for creative endeavours through copyright royalties the music industry will cease to exist.

This final point seems to be the crux of contemporary debates on music copyright. The utilitarian argument seems increasingly strained as copyright increasingly favours the industry over the artist. As Frith (2004: 185) notes, musicians make music in spite of copyright, not because of it. Nevertheless, the industry and national governments continue to pursue the doctrine that stronger copyright laws and more vehement policing of infringement are beneficial to the creative process of musicians. Although counterfeiting of music CDs and DVDs is a major international issue, investigated by customs and excise and frequently connected with the criminal underworld and international drug-trafficking, it is actually the consumers of music, the likes of you and I, who have become the targets of the industry's copyright police.

The control of intellectual property in music has led to extreme measures to protect sounds, lyrics, words, melody or arrangement. Laing (1993) notes that infringement became a significant issue in the music industry once consumers were able to technologically reproduce sound recordings. The introduction of the compact tape recorder in the 1960s meant that cheap, practical and reusable recordings could be made in the home. Fears of infringement led the industry to employ new rhetorical devices to persuade consumers to respect copyright and to desist from making copies of recorded music. Marshall (2002) notes that underlying the music industry's rhetoric around unauthorised copying is a disjuncture between art and the market. The industry's claim is that infringement damages the 'artist' and compromises their ability and motivation to create new music. The notion of the romantic author is therefore invoked to control the moral high ground of what is the rightful use of recorded music. At the same time, calls to protect the creativity of the artist and their aesthetic well-being mask the commercial principles of the music industry, which is primarily interested in profit. The industry has consistently labelled copyright infringement as 'piracy', a morally and politically loaded term which suggests criminal activity and illegality. How this rhetoric has been used over time is instructive, not least because it reveals the way in which the policing of copyright law shapes the commercial practices of the industry. With this in mind, we shall look briefly at two broad areas of copyright infringement that have come under increased censure by the industry and government authorities. These are home recording and peer-to-peer downloading of digital music files.

Home recording

The rhetoric of music companies has always been that home recording represents a form of theft. For many years, the UK trade association for the industry, the British Phonographic Industry (BPI), ran a campaign to suggest that 'Home taping is killing music'. Other trade organisations in other nations have had similar campaigns. The rise of CD burning has reignited the issue, with the level of sales of recordable CD-Rs mushrooming since 2001. Many of these fears are centred on territories with advanced communication systems and high levels of personal technology. For instance, industry figures pointed to the fact that more than 239 million CD-Rs were sold in Japan in 2002 compared to 229 million music CDs (Borland, 2003). Such figures serve the ideological interests of the major record companies and are used as weapons in the public row over the issue of home recording and infringement of copyright.

The self-serving nature of many such statistics does, however, agitate many consumers and advocates of new technologies to deliver more access and malleability of music in digital formats. Issues of fair dealing (UK) or fair use (USA) are drawn upon to argue against what many would view as the quibbling music industry. This contrary opinion holds that once a CD, record or tape has been bought, the owner should have the right to use their property as they like (Frith, 1993). As a very common practice, many would point to home taping and CD-R burning as viable mechanisms of sharing music, knowledge and culture (Lessig, 2001).

The music industry sees things differently, and for obvious reasons. The global fall in album sales is unequivocally connected with the rise of Internet file-sharing and CD burning. As we have already noted in Chapter 3, the main difference between copying old analogue formats and digital formats is the quality and ease of reproduction and the instantaneous ability to share digital content via computer networks. The development and availability of CD burners and software to manage digital music files on personal computers have certainly made the copying of music far more accessible. This is ironic given the strong lobbying and marketing expense which the music industry pumped into the introduction of CDs in the 1980s to replace vinyl as the major sound carrier. It did so in the knowledge that copyright legislation would recognise and protect digital formats. But the reality is starkly different.

The issue of home recording represents a wider economic battle between electrical hardware manufacturers, who introduce new ways of reproducing and storing music, and the record industry, which lobbies hard to protect its artists and sound recordings from piracy. The commercial struggle is given a further political dimension by the fact that the most powerful hardware companies are based in Japan, while the major record companies are based in Europe and the USA (Laing, 1993). In the 1980s, one resolution to lost royalties due to home taping was to introduce a levy on blank tapes and recording hardware. The levy provided a mechanism of remunerating artists for market imperfections caused by the common practice of copying tapes. The tape levy was also a means of safeguarding the public's fundamental rights to privacy, as they were allowed to use recordings as they saw fit in their own homes. The latest EU Copyright Directive leaves individual member states to decide what levy schemes, if any, are introduced. While most European countries have introduced legislation on home taping, the UK and Ireland have abstained from operating levies because an additional tax on electrical goods and tapes would, it is argued, destabilise the market and prove politically sensitive to the British and Irish electorate. This has meant that UK artists cannot claim royalties on tape levies raised in other countries, because similar legislation is not enforced in Britain.

A further method of protection has been to control the release of pre-recorded music on to new formats. Digital Audio Tape (DAT) was viewed as a potential threat to the relatively recent introduction of CDs. DATs allowed digital reproduction, resulting in perfect copies time and again. A prerequisite of introducing new 'sound carriers' to the consumer market has been the ability to buy prerecorded music as an incentive to buy the necessary hardware to play it on. Record companies abstained from releasing titles on DAT, and the mass consumer market was snuffed out in an instant. Instead, DAT became the standard format of record producers for storing master copies with flexibility and ease of use. The introduction of minidisks posed similar questions. Changes to the market structure of the music industry, with hardware manufacturers taking over or merging with content providers (i.e. Sony and CBS Records), have added to the complexity of what, when and where prerecorded formats are innovated and released.

The proliferation of CD writers in personal computers does appear to have shifted the terrain of personal copying to new heights. Blank CD-Rs have become increasingly affordable when sold in multiple packs in supermarkets and discount computer stores. When Apple relaunched its new range of colourful iMacs in the late 1990s, its marketing slogan was 'Rip. Mix. Burn'. As Lessig (2001: 9) observes, the ad campaign touched on a historical urge to turn consumers into creators, enabling Apple users to take control of their culture, to actively engage with the music they have chosen to listen to in new and creative ways. As students of popular culture would note, this is not a new phenomenon: in many ways, the concept of the cultural *bricoleur* (Hebdige, 1979), applied to the punk phenomenon and subsequently applied to the rise of hip-hop, neatly fits the practices of millions of music fans as they compile the assorted tracks of their music collections in new and innovative ways.

The music industry has sought to deal with this new phenomenon in various ways, all of which attempt to claw back control of the use of music CDs. One method of restricting private copying has been to introduce technologies that prevent or at least restrict the act of reproduction itself, such as introducing digital rights-management software into the manufacture of CDs. The industry had previously used restrictive technologies such as the Serial Copy Management System (SCMS) for DAT to permit one copy of a recording to be made but then preventing additional copies to be cloned from the master copy. In line with the principle of restricting use, in 2001 some record labels introduced copy-protected CDs that prevented the use of music CDs in personal computers. The technology (devised by Microvision's SafeAudio and Midbar's Cactus Data Shield) was illicitly brought into the mainstream sale of CDs as a means of slowing down the rate at which tracks were being 'ripped' on to PCs to be compressed into MP3 files and shared on the Internet. The software introduces digital distortions that creates audible clicks and pops when played through a computer. One side-effect of the copy-protected CD was that it also disrupted the playing of CDs on some car stereos.

The technology has been widely criticised by the computing community and music fans who simply want to listen to their CDs on their PC. The DRM software also raises issues of fair use, as it negates the common practice of making a personal copy of a CD for non-commercial uses.

As a means of combating criticism from consumers, many CDs now carry two sets of music files – one that is readable to CD players, the other carrying compressed files readable to computer drives and available for downloading on to PCs. Second session recording, as it is known, attempts to allay fears of heavy-handed protection of CDs by the major labels. The files themselves are encrypted for use on specific media players (chiefly Microsoft's Windows Media Player or Apple's iTunes), which again restrict the uses of the files once copied to a computer. The division of the original CD files with lower-quality files for copying to a computer reflects the industry's view that if copying is to be allowed for personal use under copyright legislation, then that must be a single copy of inferior quality to the original. Other initiatives include the IFPI's standardisation of a digital fingerprint on manufactured CDs that provides a unique and permanent identifier for each CD. The International Standard Recording Code (ISRC) enables the copyright holder to track the use of CDs. The IFPI cites the main purpose of this technology as a form of royalty tracking when music is electronically distributed; but it can clearly have the potential to be used to detect copyright infringement as the protected music files move from PC to PC.

The introduction of DRM into music CDs provides another instance of the deliberate imbalance of copyright law to favour the major media corporations. 'Fair use' arguments premised on the belief that users have certain rights to copyright works, particularly where they bear no commercial threat to the copyright holder, are being eroded. Instead, copyright holders are extending their rights through the use of technologically encrypted keys to lock out unauthorised use. As we are aware from Chapter 3 and the circumvention of DVD encryption, new legislation instigated by the WIPO Treaty, and carried forward in the DMCA (USA) and the European Copyright Directive, ensures that any attempts by music fans to unlock copy-protected CDs are criminal acts. Laws protecting technology now police copyright to the detriment of consumers and their own rights within copyright.

Internet file-sharing

The ability to store music digitally opened up the possibility of distributing music via computer networks. In 1993, before the Internet gained global recognition, an organisation called the Internet Underground

Music Archive began to produce short extracts of unknown bands available on the World Wide Web. The site also transferred extracts of music from major artists before they were officially released. Although the files took an age to download, the added value of the site was that it also distributed additional material and biographies about the artists involved. Artists themselves turned to the new medium, developing their own websites – the most notable being the Rolling Stones, who produced one of the first webcasts in 1994 to a small elite audience. The adventurous, pioneering spirit of those who worked in the music industry began to transfer itself to the Internet and shaped its use.

What digital networks brought to music was a new medium in which to distribute original work to a potentially global audience. Given that the music industry had a long-established international market, the Internet posed a significant threat to the control of copyright works and exclusive markets. The Internet effectively cut out manufacturers, distributors and record stores to connect, in a much more direct way, the artist and the fan. New e-commerce companies emerged to handle the new relationship between producer and consumer, seeking industry approval to license the downloading of music files. A London-based company, Cerberus, was one of the first to innovate a pay-for-use website with industry backing. Individual tracks were available to download for a small fee (15p) supplemented by a royalty payment to the record company.

But the revolution in the transfer of music via the Internet came with the dual innovation of compressed music files, primarily the MP3 format, and the creation of peer-to-peer networks that connected individual computers via central nodes enabling the sharing of personal computer files. MP3 had its genesis in the MPEG movie format used for the digital storage of audio-visual material. The key software in creating MP3 music was a 'ripper' that generated files in compressed formats that were one-tenth the size of that used on a standard CD. The format grew from people swapping music files on the Internet, via e-mail, and exploded in use once dedicated MP3 websites began to appear, most notably MP3.com. One noticeable absentee from the new mode of music distribution in the formative period of MP3 was the music industry. As one early pioneer of MP3 music pronounced in 1997:

> The music business has always controlled the technology and the distribution [...] and they've always ripped us off by making us buy everything again in new formats – they did it with CDs, and they'll do it again with DVD audio. This is the first time we've beaten them, because we've got a new system they don't dare use. This time they have to catch up with us. (Quoted in the *Daily Telegraph*, 2 September 1997)

In the late 1990s, a host of websites with MP3 downloads emerged along with the portable hardware to store and play MP3 files. MP3.com innovated the notion of pushing new artists to open up access to their music for downloading to subscribers of its service. In January 2000, it introduced a new service called MyMP3.com that allowed music fans to stream music to their desktops from the MP3.com servers as long as they already personally owned a copy of the CD. The idea was that you could listen to 'your' music on any computer connected to a network without the hassle of carrying your CD collection with you wherever you went. The problem for this cunning innovation was of course that although you might own the hard copy of a CD when you buy it from a store, you do not own the copyright. The law states that you may use your CD in any way you see fit, but you do not have a right to do what you like with the music contained on it. Later in 2000, MyMP3.com was taken to court for infringement of copyright by the Recording Industry Association of America (RIAA) on behalf of five of the major record companies, EMI, WMG, BMG, Sony and UMG. The case revolved around the unlicensed use of 80,000 albums on the MyMP3.com database which were available to download from its site. All except UMG settled out of court with undisclosed terms in the region of $20 million each for licence agreements. In September 2000, MyMP3.com was found to be liable for violation of copyright and was asked to pay $25,000 per CD from the 10,000 albums which UMG claimed had been infringed. MP3.com had tried to introduce a new value chain into the music industry, connecting artists directly with the consumer, cutting out the middlemen of record companies, distributors and record stores. However, as more recent digital download services have discovered, breaking the established chain between artists and consumers has been incredibly complex due to industry stubbornness (Wallis, 2004). MP3.com was soon bought out by the Universal Music Group, who then folded the original company. The URL changed hands to CNetworks, the interactive content publisher, which uses MP3.com as a portal to access online music from various sources.

The main challenge to the established distribution of music came with the innovation of peer-to-peer technologies, made most famous by the file-swapping service Napster. Napster was the brainchild of nineteen-year-old programmer Shawn Fanning, who devised the software to enable him to share music files with his friends. Peer-to-peer technology basically returned the increasingly centralised system of the Internet, in the guise of the World Wide Web, to the end user of networks. As Fanning argued, the idea was to cut out the need to find information via a central server and instead to find information that's housed nearest to you, because 'if it's already on the computer of the kid down the hall, why travel halfway around the world to retrieve it?' (Merriden, 2001: viii). The principle behind Napster was one of sharing digital music in the MP3 format, although other types of files could also be downloaded. The Napster software, downloaded for free from the website, allowed users to 'rip' music stored on a traditional CD and then be listed on a Napster server for others to download. The website gained recognition for its maverick approach to music on the Internet and soon built up a huge user base after its launch in 1999. However, as the network mushroomed with a reported 60 million users worldwide (cnn.com, 2001), the US music industry soon brought an injunction to prevent further copyright infringement.

Litigation for infringement of copyright was brought by the RIAA in December 1999, with subsequent action taken by the rock group Metallica. Acting on behalf of the major record labels, the RIAA viewed the file-sharing Internet site as a 'haven of music piracy'. The initial case was brought in a Los Angeles district court, under Judge Marilyn Hall Patel. Her ruling in July 2000 imposed an injunction on the website and the insistence that all copyrighted works be removed from the service. However, two days later, the ruling was suspended on appeal to the Supreme Court. The media coverage that followed the initial case fuelled the notoriety of the website, which claimed that it was registering 250,000 new customers per week during the second half of 2000.

The US Court of Appeal, with three judges presiding, passed its judgement in February 2001. Like the district court before it, the 9th Circuit Court of Appeals found little sympathy for the Internet music-swapping service Napster, finding it liable for both contributory and vicarious copyright infringement. The decision chipped away at the famous holding in the 'Betamax' case, where the Supreme Court held that the movie studios could not outlaw a technology (VCRs) that was capable of substantial non-infringing uses. The appellate court then ordered Napster to police and control its systems to prevent future infringement and sent the case back to the district court for specific rulings about how Napster must rewrite its software to meet the court's requirements. This ruling marks a stark departure from the Supreme Court's standard for third-party liability in Betamax, where knowledge that VCRs would be used for some infringement was irrelevant. In Betamax, the Supreme Court held that allowing copyright holders to ban devices capable of substantial non-infringing uses would go beyond the power of copyright monopoly, regardless of whether the creators knew that their devices would be used to infringe copyrights. Although the appellate court disagreed with the district court and held that Napster was capable of substantial non-infringing uses, it nonetheless held that the Betamax defence was unavailable to Napster because of its actual knowledge of specific infringement and unwillingness to prevent that infringement.

According to the court, contributory liability may potentially be imposed to a file-sharing technology provider which receives reasonable knowledge of specific infringing files, knows or should know that such files are available on the system, and fails to act to prevent viral distribution of the works.

Despite Napster's lack of a business model, the court found that it benefited financially because the availability of the music acted as a draw for future customers. The final ruling by the district court in March 2001 modified the injunction to demand that Napster remove all copyrighted material from its website and that it operate a filter system to track any copyright material passing through its portal. However, the filtering software proved less than efficient and led to its users changing the names of files (e.g. Madonna became 'Madona') to outmanoeuvre the scrutiny of files being downloaded. Latterly, Napster added further filters that detected sounds rather than names of files through a technology called 'sound fingerprinting'. The website also attempted to pay off the major record labels with a compensatory offer of $1bn each. The money was to act as a licence for the use of copyright material, but was flatly turned down by the media companies. Crippled by legal fees and the loss of its user base that had fled to newer, less regulated file-sharing services like KaZaa, Napster filed for bankruptcy. In a bitter irony, its assets were bought by the media corporation Bertelsmann, which relaunched Napster as a legitimate download service in spring 2004, including a new download chart introduced in September 2004. For many of its former users, its brand had become tarnished as it became subsumed under the wing of the corporate music industry that it had once undermined.

The original Napster claimed that the swapping of music files taken from an individual's own CD collection equated with the swapping of taped CDs between friends. In trying to defend itself in a case brought by A & M Records, Napster failed to convince the judge that the US Audio Home Recording Act 1998 on home taping also applied to downloading files from the Internet. What is interesting about the case is that copyright was originally designed as a mechanism for protecting publishers from the piracy of other publishers, not, as in these cases, from artists or users of copyrighted materials. It could be argued that individuals should have the right to make use of copyrighted work as they desire, except for when they are 'competing for profits' (Frith, 1993). Digital technology blurs the boundaries of production, distribution and consumption to such an extent that it no longer becomes clear who is violating what.

The industry's claim that illegal downloading of MP3 files was harming musicians and creativity fell on deaf ears. This is partly because most music fans most of the time will access music as cheaply and as quickly as possible. It is also because many music fans see through the rhetoric of the industry and see that the industry and its leading stars are making plenty of money, thank you very much. However, where does this leave musicians struggling to make a living? How important is protecting copyright for them? How does digital distribution of music fit into their economic sustainability? Toynbee (2004) notes that, in terms of creativity, copyright can be viewed as a burden to new, up-and-coming talent. Instead, innovation in music is more likely to be derived from what he calls 'phonographic orality', the idea that all music lends and draws upon other musical works, than it is from copyright as a key motivator for innovation. So, on the count of damaging creativity, the industry's fears that digital downloads impact on creativity are arguably unfounded. On an economic level, we can clearly see that young musicians might well view the protection of their rights as an important mechanism for surviving economically, but all too often are forced into signing recording contracts that effectively remove their ability to control how their rights are used (Greenfield and Osborne, 2004). If digital downloading is to become the standard economic transaction between artists and music consumers, new ways of balancing the rights of both parties may need to be innovated.

Conclusion

As we have discovered, the economics of the music industry are premised on the ability to leverage a 'basket of rights' to generate revenue and retain exclusive rights of distribution and sale of recorded music. In spite of new efficiencies in the collection of rights by collecting societies, enhancing the pool of royalties to be shared by musicians, songwriters and others, the balance of power in the music industry remains perversely skewed in favour of the major record labels. Only a handful of members benefit from the collection of performing rights or mechanical rights, and the industry mops up most of the neighbouring rights for itself. For example, a mere 10 per cent of composers receive 90 per cent of the money redistributed by the PRS. Such figures negate the argument that copyright acts as an incentive to create music. Economic pressures, brought about by complex shifts in culture and global commerce, mean that a mere 5 per cent of albums return a profit for the major record labels. However, the bulk of their marketing resources and energy is pumped into these few artists under the philosophy of 'winner takes all'. The outcome of this process is a narrowing of the album releases year on year and increased barriers to access for new talent. This enables music companies to negotiate contracts on their terms which are invariably disadvantageous in terms of future income and promotion of new talent (Greenfield and Osborne, 2004). Ironically, as the potential to distribute music with relative ease via digital networks has become a reality, the industry itself, scared of the loss of control of music copyright, is shoring up the potential availability and uses that digital music affords.

The enduring legacy of the Napster case is that it raised public awareness of copyright issues, at least in the sense that what the public thought was free and open access to music for non-commercial uses was in fact deemed 'piracy' by the record industry. The demise of Napster merely displaced peer-to-peer file-sharing to other destinations and shall continue to do so until the industry itself finds new ways to open up access to music which it increasingly locks away behind copyright laws and encryption technology.

To briefly return to the inroads of Apple within the music industry, to a certain extent the story has turned full circle. Apple, through its digital download service and proprietary music software iTunes, has blazed a trail in innovating the digital downloading of music. Its US service approached more than 100 million downloads in its first year of operation (2003), and a similar success story appeared to be emerging in Europe on its launch in June 2004. Apple persuaded the music industry to license their music to the service due to its ease of access and proprietary system that continued to protect digital files once downloaded. Therefore, the files, stored in a format known as Advanced Audio Coding (AAC) and considered superior in quality to MP3, are attached with encrypted software called FairPlay that enables multiple copying to standard CDs or to the portable music player iPod but restricts the sharing of tracks to three authorised computers. This is aimed at preventing peer-to-peer file-sharing. Apple's head start in music downloading has been driven not so much by its trademark innovative design, particularly the 'must have' iPod, but its ability to find a business and technological solution that allays the fears of the recording industry. Apple's goal, partly achieved with the availability of iTunes on standard PCs with Windows operating systems, is to become the *de facto* supplier of digital music downloads. The final twist is that the business model is not based on generating profits from the unit price of music; rather, it is in the sale of hardware (iPods) and the iTunes software that income is generated. Again, the historical links to previous technologies are instructive. Much like the origin of the BBC, formed by a consortium of wireless manufacturers in order to provide content to fill the airwaves and attract new consumers, Apple is attempting to create a new generation of digital-music lovers who can store and use their music in new and innovative ways but sanctioned under licence by the recording industry.

Study questions

Should the swapping of music files be viewed as fair use of a music product once it has been bought in the form of a CD? Is it just like home taping and swapping tapes with friends – and if not, why not?

Further reading

Frith, S. and L. Marshall (eds) (2004), *Music and Copyright*, 2nd edn, Edinburgh: Edinburgh University Press.
Passman, D. (2002), *All You Need to Know about the Music Business*, London: Penguin Books.

Relevant websites

The Performing Rights Society – http://www.prs.co.uk/
The Mechanical Copyright Protection Society – http://www.mcps.co.uk/
Phonographic Performance Ltd – http://www.ppluk.com/
Performing Artists Media Rights Association – http://www.pamra.org.uk/
The Musicians Union – http://www.musiciansunion.org.uk/welcome.shtml
Video Performance Limited – http://www.musicmall.co.uk/vpl/mm_design.nsf/splash?openpage

5 Broadcasting rights to sport

High Court action, debt-laden media corporations, threatened strike action, collapsed pay-TV ventures and attempts to woo audiences with a puppet monkey: the marriage of the media and sport has taken some peculiar turns at the start of the new century. For most people, most of the time, sport means media sport. The media set our parameters of what sport means in society, and they offer our most regular contact with sporting heroes. Sport is one of the most cherished forms of media content, and broadcasting rights to access sporting events have become a central feature of the media economy.

The industries of sport and the media are inexorably intertwined. One cannot pick up a newspaper, watch television news or browse the Internet without noticing the ubiquitous nature of sport across all media forms. As new information and communication technologies are innovated at an incredible pace, so the appetite for sports content follows closely behind. There can be little doubt that the relationship between the two industries has been transformed in the multichannel age. However, the promised new audiences for digital television platforms, broadband Internet and third-generation (3G) mobile phones and heightened streams of income for sport have largely failed to materialise. If we take the case of the most popular media sport, football, more clubs are in debt than ever before as player salaries escalate and pay-TV channels struggle to sustain their investment in the sport in the wake of an advertising slump and a slowdown in new subscribers (Boyle and Haynes, 2004).

A willingness to pay for the pleasure of watching sport has been long established. The process of professionalisation in many sports had occurred before the turn of the twentieth century. Large spectator sports were, therefore, a natural home for emerging forms of media, whether it be the press, film newsreel, radio or television. Sport created a ready-made audience; and the media, in particular television, has used the spectacle of sport to leverage an audience and capture the imagination of its viewers. Sport is ready-made for television. Its use by television adds an important dimension to media rights, because how we value sport in society has a direct effect on the licensing, acquisition, distribution and ultimate consumption of sport. Issues of power, politics and influence are brought to the fore because sport is often viewed as being precious to a nation's cultural heritage, and indeed is promoted as such by the media. Unlike any other area of media rights, the negotiation of sports rights takes on a peculiarly public character. The sale of sports rights can engender embittered public debate between different parties with different vested interests, some of which are laced with economic reasoning, but most of which are cultural in nature. People tend to have more knowledge and opinion on the issue of sports rights than on any other aspect of media rights. As we shall discuss below, this is largely due to the place of sport in the culture of broadcasting, where there has been a general reluctance to pay for something that used to be free (or, at least, paid for by the licence fee).

This reasoning also has a wider international resonance, as many nations copied the method of outside broadcasting innovated by the BBC, taking on board the ideological premise of sharing the experience of sporting events with the national audience. As the broadcasting landscape across Europe and North America has changed over the past fifty years, one element has remained constant: the need for sport as primary content. Television stations have risen and fallen on their ability to attract key sports, and with them an emotionally dedicated audience. Sports rights can be, and usually are, the flagship and distinguishing factor of a television station's brand identity, and are lost at their peril. Understanding why sport is so important demands a knowledge of how the relationship between sport and broadcasting has developed and how the power relations between sports authorities and broadcasters have dynamically changed over time.

A brief history of televised sport in the UK

BBC Television officially began broadcasting to a select few in November 1936. Outside broadcasts from sport soon followed in 1937–8, with many 'firsts' from Wimbledon, Twickenham, Wembley and the Oxford–Cambridge Boat Race. Initially, no fee was paid by the BBC, forged on the back of Lord Reith's public-service philosophy of broadcasting to the nation. But, in the immediate post-war period, this policy met a level of resistance from sports administrators (in 1944, several sporting bodies joined forces to form the Association for the Protection of Copyright in Sport). Their main concern, and one which still prevails today, was the threat of television to actual attendance at sporting events. In particular, they feared the 'rediffusion' of television transmissions in public places (i.e. cinemas, community halls and pubs). From the 1950s, the BBC agreed to pay sports administrators a token 'facility fee' for the right to televise their sport. Organisations like the Football League maintained a ban on 'live' coverage of games, but did allow filmed highlights of matches on Saturday evenings. Live broadcasts from football were restricted to the FA Cup, internationals (boosted by the innovation of 'Eurovision' in 1954) and an assortment of amateur and friendly matches played outwith the auspices of the League under floodlight, which allowed clubs to negotiate their own terms for broadcast rights (Haynes, 1999).

BBC and ITV: a cosy duopoly

The arrival of commercial television in the UK in 1955 generated a new, competitive approach to the coverage of sport by the BBC. Pre-empting the decline of the BBC's monopoly, in 1954 the BBC launched a new sports omnibus programme, *Sportsview*, presented by Peter Dimmock. The programme adopted an innovative magazine format that combined filmed material with studio presentation and interviews. There was much emphasis placed on sporting 'personalities', with the imperative of winning support from a broad 'family audience'. *Sportsview*, broadcast on Wednesday evenings, was soon joined by its sister programmes *Sports Special*, presented by Kenneth Wolstenholme on Saturday evenings from 1955, and later by *Grandstand*, presented by David Coleman, which became the BBC's flagship sports programme from 1958. These programmes gave the BBC an unrivalled foothold both in outside-broadcast production from sport and, more importantly, in its relations with the governing bodies of sport, which received no more than token remuneration for the licence to televise their sports.

Conversely, ITV franchises faced an upward struggle in their attempts to televise sport. In his history of ITV companies, Sendall (1982) notes two main restrictions for the networks' inroads into sports rights. Firstly, the regional structure of the ITV franchises made efficient and centralised planning of programmes difficult; secondly, the commercial nature of ITV did not quite fit with the traditional amateur ethics and commercial reticence of many sports organisations.

However, by the late 1960s, the ITV companies had established a centralised Sports Network and introduced *World of Sport* to challenge *Grandstand* on Saturday afternoons and LWT's *The Big Match* to rival *Match of the Day*. ITV still held a minority position in televising sport in the 1970s, and relied heavily on cheap imported sports programming from North America (including cliff diving from Acapulco!). However, as a member of the European Broadcasting Union (EBU), ITV did broadcast from global sports events like the World Cup and the Olympic

Games. On such occasions, ITV and the BBC would agree on a policy of 'alternation' which allowed each channel to broadcast live from the World Cup without direct competition from the other. Bilateral agreements were also used in the negotiation of rights for domestic football. This 'cosy duopoly' meant that the broadcasters could avoid competition for exclusive rights and keep the price of TV rights for football suppressed (a deal struck in 1983 was worth a meagre £8 million to the Football League).

However, by the 1980s, ITV had begun to pursue exclusivity in its football coverage. First, it forced the BBC to alternate its traditional Saturday-evening slot, and then in 1988 it brokered a deal worth £44 million over four years. There were several factors which led to this break from British television sporting tradition. With the prospect of broadcasting deregulation on the horizon towards the end of the 1980s, the competitive bidding for TV rights to sport emerged, with new television channels and services entering the British television environment (Channel 4, Sky and British Satellite Broadcasting). The Football League and its member clubs were under increased economic pressure during the 1980s due to falling attendances (with the blight of hooliganism and competition from other leisure activities). Moreover, the decline in popularity of edited highlights had led to limited experimentation with live broadcasts of League matches on Friday nights and Sunday afternoons. The potential of live football to woo audiences, meeting the needs of ITV's advertisers and sponsors, proved a tremendous fillip to the wider exposure of the sport on television.

Sport as 'dish driver': the rise of subscription sport

Attempts to soften the ideological importance of public-service broadcasting began with the 1984 Cable and Broadcasting Act, which was subsequently superseded by the 1990 Broadcasting Act. Both sought to free up the regulatory framework of British television to introduce a new era of British television culture firmly rooted in the private sector. However, both BSB and Sky had a faltering start in establishing satellite distribution and programming. Both companies were 'bleeding' money at alarming rates because of the high costs of setting up pay-TV services and subsidising the cost of the technology required to decode the satellite signal (Horsman, 1997). The two companies merged in 1990 to form BSkyB, with Rupert Murdoch's News Corporation Group majority shareholders with 40 per cent.

Football had also been undergoing a major modernising process after the disasters at Heysel, Bradford and Hillsborough. In June 1991, the Football Association published its *Blueprint for the Future of Football*, which pre-empted a move to dislocate the top flight of English football away from the Football League under the auspices of a newly appointed FA Premier League. This move was wholly generated by the need to rebrand the game for television and sponsors. After a protracted series of negotiations by the chairmen of the new Premier League and the television companies (ITV and BSkyB), the rights were awarded to BSkyB for the unprecedented amount of £304 million over five years, with exclusive rights to sixty live matches a season, and highlights going to the BBC.

What were the consequences of the BSkyB deal?

Throughout the 1990s, there was an influx of cash into football and other sports captured by the satellite broadcasters' dedicated sports channels. Initially, much of this money contributed to the modernisation of stadia required under the 1991 Football Spectators Act (prompted by the 1989 Taylor Report on the Hillsborough Tragedy). Later, a large proportion of the income received from television dropped straight into the pockets of leading sports stars. The wage bill of leading football clubs reached 60 to 70 per cent of their annual turnover. The Premier League originally promised more evenly distributed television rights fees based on wider exposure of all clubs to live coverage. At the same time, financial reward would be linked to performance, enabling successful clubs to retain more of the television revenues. As the leading clubs such as Arsenal, Manchester United and Liverpool used television income to buy more and more overseas players to bulk up their squads, with the perennial desire to compete in the Champions' League, so those clubs out of the top flight found it increasingly difficult to compete. The 'top-heavy' nature of the Premier League led some clubs to gamble their future financial stability in the hope of joining the European elite. Leeds United, for example, was controlled by a plc who used City investment and the securitisation of future television and season-ticket revenue to buy success. However, the club gambled the capital investment on players and inflated salaries that led to an unsustainable wage burden and debt spiralling towards £80 million. The burden of interest payments ultimately drove the club close to administration, and between 2002 and 2003 the club was forced into a fire sale of leading players. The diminished squad subsequently failed to secure Premiership status, being relegated in 2004. Other clubs have been more fortunate and have attracted new investment to stabilise the financial mismanagement brought on by negligent spending on players. In the summer of 2003, Russian billionaire Roman Abramovich bought Chelsea FC for £140 million and proceeded to spend a further £100 million on some of the world's leading players. Such benevolence is increasingly rare in sport and is a rare counterweight to the mounting debt in which many sports clubs have found themselves.

In the mid to late 1990s, media companies also became interested in actually owning a piece of football. In 1998, BSkyB attempted to buy Manchester United for more than £600 million. The move was an attempt by the satellite broadcaster to control the rights value of one of the world's leading sports brands. The approach emerged in conjunction with an Office of Fair Trading investigation into the collective sale of broadcasting rights by the Premier League clubs. If the OFT were to find the deal anti-competitive, BSkyB would be faced with losing its exclusive rights to screen the Premiership, and deals with individual clubs would become the focus of rights sales. As owners of Manchester United, BSkyB would be able to secure rights to the dominant, most widely supported club in the UK, with the broader commercial opportunities that this would bring. If the OFT decided to allow the collective sale of rights, as the owners of Manchester United BSkyB would potentially have a powerful voice on the Premier League board. The takeover was referred to the Monopolies and Mergers Commission, based on fears that the vertical integration of the UK's leading pay-TV channel with England's premier club would be contrary to the public interest. Fan groups and a section of United shareholders protested against the takeover and ultimately persuaded the Department of Trade to block the sale (Walsh and Brown, 1999). After this affair, FA regulations barred media companies from owning more than 9.9 per cent of any club where they had shares in more than one team.

Picking up the pieces: sport on terrestrial television

An interesting development during the migration of premium sports rights to BSkyB has been a series of collaborations between the satellite broadcaster and traditional terrestrial broadcasters. From 1992 to 2001, ITV was left smarting over the BBC's collusion with BSkyB to secure secondary rights to edited highlights of the Premier League. Throughout this period, *Match of the Day* enjoyed something of a renaissance, the BBC building the programme as a brand with its own magazine, premised on the growing reputation of smooth-talking presenter Des Lynam. ITV fought back by capturing rights to live UEFA Champions League football and crucially wresting the rights to Premier League highlights (2001–4) for £183m. Central to ITV's strategy on the launch of its new flagship football programme *The Premiership* was to schedule the highlights package during Saturday prime time on ITV1.

Fronting the programme was Lynam, poached from the BBC the previous year. Its first outing received 4.3m viewers, an improvement on

Match of the Day's waning audience the previous season, but well below the expected audience for ITV1 on a Saturday evening. Unfortunately, a special edition of *The Weakest Link* on BBC1 gained 6.7m viewers as it matched up against *The Premiership*, whose ratings dropped off dramatically throughout September and October 2001. The programme was slammed in the press for its unpolished and hurried presentation, damaging the reputation of Lynam, who ironically had been a long-standing critic of *MOTD*'s late-night slot. In November 2001, the programme was humiliatingly replaced by the return of *Blind Date* and pushed back to 10:30pm. The misjudgement by ITV must have upset the Premier League and their new sponsors Barclaycard. The channel had mistakenly thought that football was family viewing, when in fact football largely attracts a niche market predominantly made up of male sports fans.

Throughout the 1990s, the BBC was hit by a series of losses to its sports portfolio. Ryder Cup golf, test-match cricket and Formula One motor racing were among the main events to fall out of the Corporation's hands. However, since 2001, the BBC has rekindled a competitiveness for key sports rights after a decade of losing out to BSkyB and other terrestrial broadcasters. This strategic change was due in part to its then new Director General, Greg Dyke, who championed the use of sport to bolster the Corporation's public-service remit. This included a return to live boxing, including the first free-to-air screening of world heavyweight champion Lennox Lewis and an exclusive ten-fight deal with Olympic champion Audley Harrison. The move back to televised boxing after a hiatus of more than ten years away from the sport was heavily criticised by some – not least for the paucity of the boxing on show. However, the reintroduction of boxing as well as increased coverage of athletics and other sports outside of the dominant game of football at least showed a commitment by the BBC to maintain its position as a leading sports broadcaster. More recently, the BBC regained the rights to screen highlights of Premier League football from 2004–5 for £105 million as well as renewing its long-standing coverage of the FA Cup.

The fallout of ITV Digital

Although the Premier League has secured most of pay-TV's riches, the Football League also negotiated a lucrative three-year deal with the digital terrestrial broadcaster ITV Digital (then named OnDigital) for £315m to help support the launch of the ITV Sports Channel in the autumn of 2001. Launched in 1998, ITV Digital was the UK's first digital terrestrial broadcaster, a direct competitor to BSkyB's digital satellite service. Given the seemingly buoyant position of televised football, exemplified by BSkyB's experience, the Football League deal did not raise too many eyebrows among media sports analysts at the time. On the surface, the deal presented a boon for the smaller clubs cast adrift from the riches of the Premier League.

However, signs that broadcasters were beginning to question the value of football rights surfaced when cable network NTL reneged on a £326m contract to screen forty Premier League matches on a pay-per-view (ppv) basis starting from the 2001–2 season. The sums basically did not add up. NTL's subscriber base was too low, while take-up of ppv football in the UK was unknown and proved a considerable gamble, given that sixty-six matches were already sidelined for BSkyB. Eventually, the ppv rights were resold to a consortium of pay-TV channels – BSkyB, NTL, Telewest and ITV Digital – for the significantly reduced sum of £181m. To date, viewing figures for ppv games have been alarmingly low, and boxing has been the only real benefactor of this method of delivery.

Worse was yet to come. In March 2002, Carlton Communications and Granada, joint owners of ITV Digital, placed the channel into administration due to the burden of nearly £1bn of debt. Partly underlying this move was an outstanding payment of £178m to the Football League as part of the three-year deal. As the news was announced, the Football League threatened to sue the digital broadcaster for £500m, while ITV Digital attempted to table a compromise of £50m to pay off the remainder of its contract. Reports that as many as thirty clubs would face liquidation if ITV Digital did not honour its contract soon turned to anger over Carlton and Granada's handling of the situation. Club chairmen, the Professional Footballers' Association (PFA), managers and fans all poured scorn on the beleaguered channel.

The ITV Digital collapse ultimately hurt football more than the media corporations, with many clubs remaining threatened with bankruptcy. The clubs did manage to redeem some revenue from their television rights with a much-depleted offer from BSkyB in July 2002 worth £95m over four years, but much of the financial damage had already been done. The ITV Digital fiasco led many media sports commentators to conclude that the boom in television sports rights had reached a ceiling. Indeed, as we shall see, the football authorities and clubs began to brace themselves for significant reductions in the amount of rights fees they could leverage as negotiations for the next round of broadcasting rights got under way.

Regulation of TV sports rights: competition issues

The collapse of ITV Digital left BSkyB with a near-monopoly in the pay-TV sector and an unparalleled position in terms of capturing premium sports rights. In December 2002, the European Commission competition directorate DG4 opened proceedings against the English Premier League regarding the restrictive nature of the live television agreements it had with BSkyB. The spotlight turned to the collective sale of rights, exclusive agreements and their negative implications for broadcast markets and consumers. The EC argued that collective agreements restrict the number of games available to subscribers, and were keen to explore the possibility of all games being opened up to the multichannel broadcasting environment, including the Internet. A similar process had already taken place regarding the sale of rights to the UEFA Champions League, and now the EC's focus shifted to the domestic markets of top-flight football in England and Germany.

Central to this debate is the ability of clubs to trade some of their media rights individually. With the rise of new media outlets, many clubs now have their own television channels or broadband services. As the barriers to entry into the media marketplace decrease, so the competition for rights increases. This is increasingly important for clubs such as Manchester United with a global brand that could potentially sell new media subscription services to millions of supporters around the world. In the bidding process for the 2004–7 television rights, the Premier League under the watchful eye of EC regulators created four packages of live rights with a total of 138 games up for grabs. However, BSkyB won all four tenders in a combined offer of just over £1 billion. The Premier League were happy that they had adhered to the demands of the EC regulators by increasing the number of games available in more live packages. But ultimately there was only one UK broadcaster who could afford them, namely BSkyB. In October 2003, the European regulators ruled that the Premier League tender had not been fairly contested. It instructed BSkyB to resell one of the four packages that would be sublicensed to another channel, thereby breaking Sky Sports' exclusivity on the Premiership.

The ruling was not well received by either the Premier League or Sky executives, who saw the leakage of eight Premiership games as undermining the value of the rights they had just bought. In April 2004, sealed bids for the fourth tranche of rights were taken, but the amounts bid by the BBC, ITV, Channel 5 and Setanta Sports fell well below a minimum reserve price per match (reported to be £1.5 million) set by BSkyB in agreement with EC regulators. Sky Sports held on to exclusive live rights for another three years. The competition authority's failure to force a change to BSkyB's dominance in Premier League rights was a considerable blow given its efforts to break up the satellite broadcaster's monopoly of live coverage since 1992. However, the next rights sale due in 2007 would come under more pressure to be divided among at least two broadcasters, as had been the case with Champions' League rights from the 2003–4 season. Moreover, the pressure to ensure an open market for televised sports rights has also led to a decrease in the timescale of rights packages, with most deals expiring after three years.

Cultural citizenship and the listed events

Although competition issues are increasingly important in the regulation of sports rights, there is another area of media policy that regulates the availability of certain broadcasting rights to sport and effectively reduces competition. The concept of 'listed events' has been around since the 1950s, when competition for television rights to sport first emerged between the BBC and ITV. In these formative years, the idea of a protected list of events related to non-exclusivity clauses. This meant that particular sporting events deemed to be of national interest were not allowed to be covered under an exclusive rights agreement. These events, listed by the Postmaster General, included the FA Cup final, the Scottish Cup final, the Boat Race, the Derby, the Grand National, the Olympic Games, test cricket, Wimbledon, the World Cup finals and the Commonwealth Games. The list was mutually agreed by the BBC and ITV and remained a gentlemen's agreement between the two broadcasters until the list was formally written into legislation in the 1984 Cable and Broadcasting Act. As Barnett (1990: 33) notes, the philosophy of the list remained consistent throughout this period, 'that while rights holders should reap the just rewards of selling their product to television, viewers should not be deprived of access to events of national importance'.

The problem for rights holders has been that the listed events effectively restrict their ability to leverage higher rents for the exclusive coverage of their sports. As the era of multichannel pay-television became a reality, some sports authorities placed increasing pressure on the government to relax the non-exclusivity clause and enable some of the listed events to be available for subscription-based channels. In the 1990 Broadcasting Act, the Conservative government maintained the list and continued to prohibit a pay-per-view service gaining exclusive rights to events of national interest, but it did enable channels to obtain exclusive rights as long as the broadcast was available to at least 95 per cent of the population. The list received further changes under Section 101 of the 1996 Broadcasting Act that divided the list into two categories. Group A events are to be available to the majority of the viewing public, free-to-air, on a non-exclusive basis (except with the prior consent of the ITC, now Ofcom) whereas 'Group B events are those events that may not be broadcast live on an exclusive basis unless adequate provision has been made for secondary coverage' (ITC, 2002a). Secondary coverage usually refers to edited highlights or delayed 'as live' coverage. The two lists as they stood in 2003 are:

Group A

The Olympic Games
The FIFA World Cup finals tournament
The FA Cup final
The Scottish FA Cup final (in Scotland)
The Grand National
The Derby
The Wimbledon tennis finals
The European Football Championship finals tournament
The Rugby League Challenge Cup final*
The Rugby World Cup final*

Group B

Cricket test matches played in England
Non-finals play in the Wimbledon tournament
All other matches in the Rugby World Cup finals tournament*
Six Nations Rugby tournament matches involving home countries**
The Commonwealth Games*
The World Athletics Championship*
The Cricket World Cup? (the final, semi-finals and matches involving
    home nations Teams?)*
The Ryder Cup*
The Open Golf Championship*

* Restrictions apply to rights acquired after 1 October 1996 except
  for those events marked by an asterisk, where the relevant date is
  25 November 1997.
** The list was amended in 2001 following the change of name of this
  event to the Six Nations Rugby Tournament. The relevant date for
  this event is therefore 24 January 2001.
  (source: ITC, 2002a)

One of the major benefactors of the 1996 Act was the England and Wales Cricket Board, which had been lobbying for a release from the strictures of the old listed events for more than a decade. In 1997, the ECB sold the rights to England's home test series in a joint deal between Channel 4 and BSkyB. The deal not only meant the end of more than forty years' association of test cricket with the BBC, but was also the first time home test matches could exclusively be covered live on a subscription sports channel. As part of the deal, BSkyB held exclusive rights to every England test held at Lords, the 'home' of world cricket. The freedom of the advertising-driven Channel 4 was also not lost on the ECB, which was able to tie in programme sponsorship that 'buffered' the coverage of test cricket between the ad breaks. The ability to leverage more commercial revenue through sponsors provided a boon to the international game in England and was greatly assisted by technological innovations in the Channel 4 coverage such as the 'hawk eye'.

Some governing bodies have, however, stuck stoutly behind the principle of free-to-air television and non-exclusivity. The IOC has retained a policy of selling the Olympic rights to channels that have a maximum reach in their relevant territories. The 'global media event' uses the philosophy of global access to foster its own ideals of a global communal event. This policy has not prevented it from leveraging enormous rights revenues in key markets, most notably the USA, where NBC has paid $5.7bn for exclusive rights from 2000 to 2012.

However, the IOC's policy is not mirrored by FIFA, the governing body of international football. Negotiations for the rights to the 2002 and 2006 World Cup finals reached an impasse in the UK when there was a huge discrepancy between the valuation of rights by Kirch Media, FIFA's European licensee, and the British broadcasters the BBC and ITV.

New media sport

In spite of the fact that BSkyB continued to dominate televised rights to top-flight sport, there are new opportunities in other areas of the media for more expansive coverage of sport. As well as the television rights in the latest Premier League deal, there is also a series of new media rights available. The EC had placed pressure on the Premier League to allocate separate broadband rights to show highlights of all the games not shown on BSkyB (some 240 games). This means that leading Internet content suppliers such as BT, AOL, Yahoo and MSN are now competing to secure rights to key sporting events. In August 2003, the Office of National Statistics estimated that one-sixth of all Internet users in the UK had access to broadband connections. This number is set to rise as more services are rolled out and prices become more competitive. Also key in this respect is the need for broadband suppliers to have quality content to entice new users from dial-up access. As in the past, sport will undoubtedly play a part in the promotional campaigns of new media services. Leading online news services such as BBCi already provide an array of audio-visual coverage of sport, and this trend is set to continue as the promise of interactive services and the integration of television coverage and the Internet are innovated.

However, we must be cautious not to over-hype the range of possibilities new media may deliver to the sports fan. The value of broadband sports rights is likely to be considerably less than television for some time. Television remains the dominant medium for most people to consume sport, and this is unlikely to change. Innovation in new media, such as the streaming of football highlights to mobile phones, is a reality but arguably remains of limited appeal. Even the market leader BSkyB has failed to realise the full potential of its digital technology. Interactive sports services remain little more than a gimmick and recoup little financial reward for the broadcaster.

Case study: Attheraces

Horse racing has been a staple diet of televised sport since the 1960s. Its main attraction to broadcasters is that it potentially fills large amounts of the schedule, all centred around one or two locations on any given day. Since 1982, Channel 4 has innovated coverage of horse racing on terrestrial television and firmly established itself as the leading advocate of racing in the UK. The connection between broadcasting and betting from horse racing has also been central to the coverage of the sport, with important information on form, fixtures, betting odds and results a key aspect of Channel 4's coverage. In the age of digital television, the proposition to marry these activities in an integrated business through coverage of the races, and multi-platform betting (via telephone, website and interactive television), have prompted the arrival of a new era of horse-racing broadcasting. In November 2001, Channel 4 joined forces with satellite broadcaster BSkyB and racecourse owner Arena Leisure to form a new media rights company to manage interactive horse-racing coverage called Attheraces (ATR). The three partners each had an equal stake in the new initiative and promptly persuaded the Racecourse Association and forty-nine of the UK's fifty-nine racecourses to sign up to a ten-year deal worth £307 million to exploit racing's media rights. The deal was struck amid fierce competition from a rival consortium backed by Carlton Television, who were then pumping millions of pounds into their new digital terrestrial platform OnDigital.

The audacious approach to exploiting the close connection between television sports rights and betting took shape in March 2002 as the channel began broadcasting. An attempt to build a channel dedicated to horse racing had appeared a year earlier with the launch of The Racing Channel, an American-owned subscription channel that broadcast races from ten racecourses owned by the company GG Media. With the arrival of ATR, The Racing Channel failed to capture a significant audience due to the paucity of fixtures available from only ten tracks. In January 2003, the channel closed, leaving GG Media to exploit its media rights exclusively to high-street bookmakers via closed-circuit relays from its courses. This left ATR with a near-monopoly on the broadcasting of UK horse racing, with the exception of the BBC, who had sublicensed some rights from ATR to the Grand National and the Derby enforced under the Listed Events legislation. ATR operated across various media formats, from its subscription channel carried on satellite and cable services, through its website, via its telephone and mobile telephone services and through a daily horse-racing programme on Channel 4.

In spite of a huge investment in the rights and advertising, the consortium faced technological setbacks in launching its interactive betting service that would enable viewers to bet through their television sets. There was a delay of six months before the service was operational, and it entered into a highly competitive marketplace in the wake of a massive boom in online betting. Although the channel's viewing figures peaked at 850,000 weekly viewers in 2003, the interactive betting service failed to capture the imagination, or money, of the viewers. The deal also came under the scrutiny of the Office of Fair Trading, which believed that the joint sale of rights to forty-nine racecourses contravened the Competition Act. By the time the OFT gave a preliminary ruling in April 2003, the financial pressure on the joint venture was beginning to tell.

Key to the success of the interactive service was the ability to generate income through betting. One aspect of this revenue stream under the rights deal was that ATR received 20 per cent of the gross profit taken from the Tote, traditionally the on-course pool betting. However, crucial to this part of the licence agreement was that the 'take-out rate' had to remain above certain set targets, and if the revenue from the Tote dipped below this threshold for more than ninety days ATR had a contractual right to renegotiate or even terminate the licence agreement. Towards the end of 2003 and into 2004, the Tote dropped its profit margin to encourage more bets; but this had an adverse effect on the 'take-out rate', moving it under the minimum limit set by ATR. The drop in Tote revenue and the lack of success of interactive betting had cost Channel 4 dearly. The channel's long-standing commitment to racing appeared to be in decline. The losses accrued from the ATR initiative meant that 4Ventures, the commercial arm of the channel, had gone from a £4.1 million profit in 2002 to a £10.1 million loss in 2003. After a crisis meeting in January 2004, the consortium decided that no more money would be paid under the media-rights agreement, and some of the £100 million already paid to the forty-nine racecourses would be subject to a rebate. ATR proclaimed that any future payment to the racecourses would be paid by a share of interactive betting revenue once the initial rights outlay had been recovered.

In March 2004, the media-rights agreement between ATR and the forty-nine racecourses was terminated as talks over a renegotiated settlement stalled. In April 2004, the OFT gave its belated ruling, concluding that the forty-nine tracks had operated anti-competitively in selling all their rights collectively, effectively enabling them to negotiate an inflated price for the rights from ATR. As the ruling suggests, the effect of the cartel was to push the cost of the rights beyond the reasonable market value to the totally unrealistic figure of £307 million, a figure some analysts believed would never be recovered by the consortium throughout the ten-year period of the deal.

The imminent collapse of ATR prompted some of the leading tracks, under the tutelage of the major racecourse consortium the Racecourse Holdings Trust, to consider setting up their own racing channel. With the prospect of no future broadcasting revenue from ATR, the owners had a firm belief that it was time to take full control of their own media rights. The technicalities of running their own channel were greatly eased by the fact that RaceTech, the company that conveyed coverage under the ATR deal, was actually owned by the Racecourse Association, the trade body of the racecourse owners. Finance for the new service, called The Horseracing Channel, came from the projected value of overseas rights sales and more realistic revenues from interactive betting. The Horseracing Channel signed up twenty-eight racecourses, thirteen from the Horseracing Holdings Trust, and initially planned to run the channel as a subscription-driven service costing £20 per month.

However, in April 2004, ATR relaunched as a new television service, now a 50:50 venture between BSkyB and Arena Leisure, who had bought out the one-third share of the original company owned by Channel 4. ATR had managed to sign up twenty-five racecourses, including the ten courses owned by GG Media (formerly on the defunct Racing Channel), for a non-subscription service running on satellite and cable platforms. They also had an established position on BSkyB's EPG, which many new channels had complained favoured Sky services. The Racecourse Holdings Trust also believed that ATR had put pressure on some of the courses with the threat of litigation regarding the 'rebate clause' in the 2001 contract. The signing of the major track Ascot to the ATR service was a great coup, and the free-to-air coverage was viewed as an important reason for its decision. The move prompted The Horseracing Channel to ditch the subscription model in order to compete with ATR on a level playing field. Both services launched in the summer of 2004 in the hope that interactive betting would eventually take off as a significant form of income to offset the huge losses incurred on both sides under the original ATR deal.

The whole episode revealed that, although sport can be vital in driving new television services and commercial enterprises, the inflated cost of rights and the subsequent pressure on profit margins ultimately jeopardise their very existence. Channel 4 ended its association with ATR by writing off £23.3 million of its initial investment in rights and very nearly withdrew from racing altogether after more than twenty years of close association. Channel 4 retained some rights to racing, including the blue-chip Cheltenham Festival event (which included the Gold Cup that attracted an audience of 1.7 million in 2004), and even renewed its proposal to introduce interactive betting via its digital channel E4. The rise of online sports betting had captured the imagination of broadcasters to use the new interactive television technology to capitalise on this gambling boon. The projected income from betting had been factored into the original £307 million rights fee which ATR paid in 2001. Ironically, the coverage provided by ATR boosted interest in racing and proved successful in boosting online betting exchanges, but it did not draw punters to bet via their television sets. The collapse of the deal brought a realisation among the racing authorities that, in the age of multichannel television, sports-rights holders have the potential to go it alone and exploit their rights independently of a third-party broadcaster. The main problem for sports-led channels is the market power of established broadcasters either through control of the EPG or in terms of long-standing brand value and viewer loyalty. However, it does enable sports authorities to potentially leverage more value from their broadcasting rights, as they are in control of the entire value chain.

Conclusion

To conclude, sport and the media remain two great wings of the entertainment industries that collude to provide some of the most memorable moments in our lives. For most people, this means the shared experience of watching the Olympic Games or the World Cup in the knowledge that millions more around the world are simultaneously indulging their own passions for sport. New media offer something less tangible in experience. Sports services are likely to be more personalised and on-demand rather than the communal secular rituals we are familiar with. But it remains early days to predict how this media market will grow and exactly how the coverage of sport will adapt to the new technology.

Sports authorities are more savvy in their dealings with broadcasters and are more likely to pursue new avenues of exploiting their media rights through various 'rights windows' such as transmission of audio and video footage via broadband networks or mobile telephony. Such developments are reliant on a viable marketplace for such technologies. The correlations between early adopters of new media technologies and the consumption of broadcast sport are instructive and have driven sport and media organisations to find new ways of delivering content. Nevertheless, there have been many failures in the 'new media age' of sport (Boyle and Haynes, 2004), and the market for media sports rights is likely to remain volatile for the foreseeable future.

Study question

Why is sport so important in the drive to introduce new television and new media platforms? Provide social, cultural and political arguments as to why (or why not) certain sporting events should be protected from pay-TV.

Further reading

Arnold, R. (2002), 'Copyright in Sporting Events and Broadcasts or Film of Sporting Events after Norowzian', in E. Barendt et al., *The Yearbook of Copyright and Media Law 2002*, Oxford: Oxford University Press.

Boyle, R. and R. Haynes (2004), *Football in the New Media Age*, London: Routledge.

Relevant websites

Sportbusiness.com – http://www.sportbusiness.com

FIFA (Marketing and Media Guidelines) – http://www.fifa.com/en/regulations/regulation/0,1584,7,00.html

UEFA – http://www.uefa.com

G14 – http://www.g14.com/intro.htm

6 Independent television producers and media rights

At its best, our TV is the envy of the world.

Tessa Jowell, Secretary of State for Culture,
Media and Sport (BTDA, 2004)

Introduction: digital television and global media markets

The arrival of digital television across three platforms – terrestrial, satellite and cable – in 1998 augured a new era of broadcasting in the UK. In 2004, over 10 million households in the UK, more than 40 per cent of the potential UK audience, had access to digital television (DCMS, 2004). The UK has trailblazed the expansion of digital television, not only in Europe but across the world. This has been heavily supported by the British government, which has consistently promised a complete 'switch-over' to digital television within the first decade of the twenty-first Century. As the quote from Culture Secretary Tessa Jowell indicates, the British have long enjoyed a proud tradition of innovation in television delivery and programming. The digital television era has proved no exception, but it is a dramatically different television landscape that is now presented compared to the oft-cited 'golden years' of British television in the 1960s and 1970s. Digital television brings with it some potentially dramatic effects on the broadcasting market beyond the mere promise of better-quality pictures and the transformative experience of interactive viewing, or 'viewsing' as it has euphemistically been labelled. The broadening of channels and choice within the television spectrum, from twenty-five channels in 1989 to more than 200 channels in 2003, also demands an increase in programme supply. Channels require content, and a new economy in television programming has emerged to fulfil this need. This may include original programming commissioned specifically for a channel; or, as is increasingly the case in the multichannel environment, the licences to broadcast programmes are internationally distributed and bought by channels to fill their schedules. The majority of the programmes bought by UK channels are from the USA at a cost of £742 million in 2002 (National Statistics, 2003). The dominance of US television exports is also emphasised by the fact that its producers and distributors receive approximately 75 per cent of revenues from all worldwide television exports (BTDA, 2003).

The USA is also by far and away the dominant player in the international sale of film rights. Year on year, approximately 90 per cent of films screened on UK cinemas originate in the USA. A similar proportion of films shown on British television also hails from Hollywood or at least has financial backing from the USA. The history of Hollywood was premised on the vertical integration of production and distribution, with further expansion into the exhibition of films in theatres. Hollywood's dominance of film from the inter-war period has gradually been expanded into other areas of popular culture, as each media innovation is delivered to the market. This has caused a steep international hierarchy in media relations between the USA and the creative and cultural industries in other nations. Where the USA is a net exporter, the UK, Japan, Germany, France and other regions are net importers of American media. The flow in cultural products and services generates international trade, but also ideological influence. This is particularly important with regard to the organising principles of the media industries themselves. In searching out new business models and operations, non-American media executives will often draw upon US media practices for inspiration and success. The hegemony of US audio-visual production and distribution practices has therefore had a profound impact on media markets and the economics of media around the world.

The UK television industry is no exception to the pressures of succeeding in a global media environment dominated by US content. The UK comes a distant second to the USA in the export of television programmes worldwide, but does dominate the rest of the world in its ability to innovate new programmes that have a resonance with international audiences. As we shall discuss later in the chapter, the rise of television formats has provided new impetus in the UK television market, and the exploitation of secondary and tertiary rights to these programme ideas has given a welcome fillip to UK distributors. Export revenue from television programme sales in 2002 was worth $754m, rising to $921m in 2003, and has shown continued growth since the late 1990s (see Table 1).

Part of the reason for the success of British programmes has been the proactive marketing of programmes in international markets by new

Table 6.1 UK television export statistics (2001–3)

Sales by territory	$ million (2001)	$ million (2002)	$ million (2003)
USA	199	284	399
Canada	22	30	31
Germany	59	44	68
France	37	40	50
Spain	22	23	32
Italy	19	18	25
Scandanavia	29	27	36
Rest of Western Europe	38	73	69
Eastern Europe	18	19	18
Australia/New Zealand	59	73	76
Latin America	24	23	16
Asia	46	59	62
Not elsewhere classified	53	39	39
Total	**624**	**754**	**921**

Source: BTDA/DCMS amalgamated figures for 2001–3.

distribution arms of the major broadcasters. BBC Worldwide, Carlton and Granada International (now merged under the ITV Company), Channel 4 International and Channel 5 International compete alongside a host of other independent programme-rights distributors in a rapidly expanding global market. Satellite offices in the USA and other regions of the world enable broadcasters and independent companies alike to leverage rights in far-flung parts of the world. The USA accounts for more than a third of UK television export earnings, more than half of this revenue generated through the sale of formats and co-productions rather than the sale of finished programmes. International television events such as MIP TV and MIPCOM also enable broadcasters to showcase their programmes and formats in the convivial surroundings of the French Riviera, where commerce and executive pleasure combine.

So what is actually being sold? As we know from our review of copyright law in Chapter 2, broadcasters maintain a set of primary rights in the programmes which they broadcast. Broadcast rights are bound by territory, therefore it is possible to license the right to broadcast programmes in other markets. The sale of licences for finished and pre-produced programmes to other markets is known as secondary rights. Once licensed, the programme is protected under the copyright legislation of the importing nation, and, if that nation is a signatory of one of the international copyright treaties or conventions, reciprocal rights in the broadcast will be available to the original broadcaster (or in many cases the associated distributor) should the programme be pirated in some way.

This 'windowing' effect of the licensing of secondary broadcast rights is a central mechanism of international trade in media markets. Other secondary rights include rental rights and sell-through rights of video and DVD, which has become the fastest-growing home entertainment technology of all time. The rise of the DVD format is due in the main to a dramatic lowering in the cost of equipment that has also prompted sales of prerecorded DVDs to climb dramatically above 140 million in 2003 (BBC, 2004). The opportunities in respect of leveraging rights revenue through such secondary markets are highly lucrative and, for independent producers, have the potential to bring in revenue far beyond the initial production fee received from broadcasters. For example, the children's television series *Bob the Builder* produced by the independent production company Hit Entertainment won wide acclaim in the UK in 2000, not only as a cartoon that pre-school children loved to watch, but also as a brand that could sell millions of videos and DVDs world-wide (including seven of the top twenty UK pre-school videos for 2000), reach number one in the UK singles charts, sell 6.5 million books, produce a live stage show with more than eighty concert performances, and be viewed in more than 130 territories around the world. Such phenomenal success is rare, but the potential to capture the imagination of the world's children and their parents and turn them into avid consumers of licensed *Bob the Builder* merchandise is the phenomenal fairytale success most independent producers dare to dream of. Moreover, international success enabled Hit Entertainment to reinvest the capital gained from secondary rights sales into owning other successful properties such as *Thomas the Tank Engine* through the acquisition of rival producers Gullane Entertainment. As we shall discover, the management of rights portfolios is central to the survival of many independent production companies with an eye on international licensing and programme sales.

As Hit Entertainment and other market leaders have shown, these further sets of rights which relate to the brand of the programme connected to the sale of merchandising known as tertiary rights are extremely valuable in the right market conditions. Tertiary rights may be associated with the exploitation of a programme in other media (books, magazines, Internet or mobile telephony) and through non-media-related merchandising (food, clothing and toys). In many cases, the brands are licensed under protection of both copyright and registered trademarks. The importance of tertiary rights to producers, broadcasters and distributors alike in the overall value chain of television programmes has received increasing attention during the 1990s and beyond. Indeed, as we shall now discover, it has been the focus of intense public policy debate as producers and broadcasters battle to control various aspects of the value chain.

State intervention in television rights markets

The necessity to compete in international markets has led to increased pressures on governments to support audio-visual industries through incentives and specific legislation. Increasingly, the state has a responsibility to encourage, foster and support the film and television industries, for both economic and cultural reasons. In the USA, there has been a close and consistent harmony between government and creative industries which has enabled US film and television producers to dominate the world market. Within the developed regions of the world, creative and cultural industries are becoming synonymous with the economic well-being of the nation. As the British film director and producer David Puttnam has argued,

> Forty years ago the symbols of national wealth and progress were steel and shipbuilding, or companies producing consumer durables. Now the rising and dominant corporate symbols of success are, almost without exception, related to information: media companies, telcos, entertainment companies, software houses ... What is clear is that as money and commodities are able to move around the globe with ever-greater ease and speed, the distinguishing characteristics of any nation or community today lie in the quality of its intellectual property; in other words, the ability of its people to use information and intelligence creatively to add substance and value to global economic activity, rather than just quantity. (Puttnam, 1997: 353)

To this end, the creative and cultural industries have been highlighted throughout the 1990s and into the new millennium by the Labour government as an important area for developing domestic and international trade. Broadly defined, they contribute revenues to the economy of more than £60bn a year, and their value to UK GDP (between 3 and 5 per cent year on year) is greater than any contribution from the UK's manufacturing industries. However, in the area of film and television production and distribution, there has been a widely held view from producers and broadcasters alike that the UK could be doing more with the range of assets and pool of talent that it has at its disposal.

In the late 1990s, the DCMS established the Creative Industries Task Force to undertake an investigation into the state of the UK industry. From an initial independent report entitled *Building a Global Audience*, an inquiry into UK television exports was established in 1999, chaired by the Secretary of State for Culture, Media and Sport, bringing together leading executives from the UK media industry. Three subgroups investigated key areas of concern: the overseas market, investment and the nature of the UK's television product ('the Right Product Group'). All three groups made recommendations to the DCMS which were published in the *Creative Industries: UK Television Exports Inquiry* (DCMS, 1999). Among the key recommendations from the Inquiry was a demand for 'a coherent government strategy on rights development and on international law relating to talent rights' (DCMS, 1999: 3). More specifically, the Investment Group recognised:

- the extent to which producers need to demonstrate the value of all secondary rights in their programmes in order to attract investors – both for the domestic and the international markets;
- the extent to which the clear separation, valuation and proper exploitation of rights is necessary to enable producers to attract meaningful levels of investment;
- the impact which changes in the arrangements for the sale of rights would have, both on the economics of broadcasting generally and on the UK television industry's performance in export markets.

The issues of media rights and their management are clearly viewed as central to the ability of film and television producers to obtain adequate financing for production. The Right Product Group also identified the need to develop incentives for production companies, in alliance with distributors, to design programmes and formats suitable for the international market. Due to the dominance of domestic needs and the commissioning practices of public-service broadcasters, producers are reluctant to look beyond the UK market. Therefore, the group recommended tax incentives or a funding scheme to 'kick-start productions designed for the international market' (DCMS, 1999: 54). Successful tax initiatives for specific genres (for example, the production of international children's programmes in Canada) were highlighted as key areas for policy and regulation. However, these tax incentives have not been implemented, and instead the focus for financing independent production has been driven by the issue of rights allocation and the exploitation of secondary and tertiary markets.

As we have discovered in earlier chapters, issues of rights can also prove a hindrance to creative industries, mainly due to the escalating cost of intellectual property rights in specific areas and developments in international policy which take an expansionist perspective in rolling out the range of rights available to the creative community. Within the audio-visual industry, the economic rents for music rights and archive footage have increased exponentially as rights holders impose prohibitive costs to protect their creative investment. As we have already seen in Chapter 4, music-rights owners – predominantly the collecting agencies –leverage their near-monopolistic control of music copyright to acquire substantial rewards from the film and television industries. Moreover, the territorial basis of rental rights has meant that the licensing of music in audio-visual media intended for the international market becomes extremely complex to negotiate and potentially expensive to overcome. In the area of policy, the rolling out of 'moral rights' under the Berne Convention and the TRIPS Agreements has also meant that performers have further control on how their work is used. This has a potential influence on where a programme might be resold and also how it might be reworked to suit international markets (that is, a performer might object to their work being re-edited or doctored for broadcast in overseas territories). Finally, the World Intellectual Property Organisation has introduced broadcast rights for audio-visual performers under the WIPO Phonogrammes Treaty, thus overriding standard contractual arrangements with programme makers and broadcasters, and providing 'equitable remuneration' for their work. The distribution of broadcasting rights down to the performer has a knock-on effect on the income stream of production companies and can lead to protracted negotiations with their artists.

These issues were carried forward to a second review of UK television exports, *Creative Industries: Out of the Box*, to 'conduct a wider examination of the television programme supply market and the relationships between broadcasters, producers, distributors and creative talent' (DCMS, 2000: 7). In particular, the Inquiry consulted on the following:

- The economic relationships in the television industry with emphasis on the different elements of the value chain, i.e. broadcasters, production and distribution companies and creative talent;
- The likely impact of new content platforms (including international channels);
- The likely impact of the changing television economy on the volumes and diversity of original content production, including the terms of the existing Independent Production Order;
- The ability of the industry to exploit fully all revenue streams including programme sponsorship (e.g. masthead programming) and merchandising;
- The allocation and retention of programme rights;
- The negotiation and development of talent-rights agreements, such as those with writers, composers, performers and musicians, with a view to identifying and making use of best-practice arrangements.

The report concluded that a lack of competition between buyers of programmes was a key barrier to a flourishing independent sector. Among its many recommendations, the report proposed the rigorous enforcement of the 25 per cent independent production quota which should be policed by a single regulatory body. As we shall see, these recommendations regarding the value chain of television production would receive further ratification by a wholesale review of programme supply by the ITC and the establishment of the Office of Communications, Ofcom, under the 2003 Communications Act.

What is clear from these initiatives is that the value of media rights and how they are organised is paramount to the development of national and international audio-visual markets. An important question to ask is whether or not it also leads to a diverse range of creative talent and a related innovation in cultural production. Part of the answer lies again in the ability of creative producers to receive adequate remuneration for their creative endeavours. In the UK, there are two interesting developments in this area, both of which highlight the conflicting nature of how media rights are controlled and exploited in the chain of producers, distributors, broadcasters and other intermediaries. The first is the lobbying from independent production companies to break monopolistic tendencies in the international trade of audio-visual content, and the second is the pressure from film and television directors to receive royalty payments for the sale or licensing of rights in secondary markets.

The ITC Programme Review and the Communications Act 2003

As the level of multichannel households in the UK moved towards 50 per cent of the national television audience between 2001 and 2002, the pressure to reassess the supply of independent programming to both established broadcasters and the new digital channels and the balance of how rights were assigned to each side became a central focus of the Labour government's new communications policy. In August 2002, the government requested a review of programme supply by the Independent Television Commission in order to gain a substantive overview of the economics of national and international markets and the 'efficacy of the independent production quota' (ITC, 2002b: 2). The ITC conducted an extensive review of available market-research data, took more than forty submissions from the industry and trade associations and held an industry seminar to gauge the general feeling among the production sector and the broadcasters. The ITC panel was chaired by Bob Philis, former Deputy Director General of the BBC and chief executive of the Guardian Media Group. The review emphasised why a buoyant independent production sector was needed in the UK, and centred on concerns for both competition and the public interest. First, it would provide a varied and economically efficient supply of programmes to viewers. Second, it would develop competition among broadcasters and enable the multichannel environment to grow. Third, it provides the basis for a thriving secondary market in programmes and the exploitation of rights in international markets. Fourth, the capital invested in the supply of independent programming could help foster creative industries in the nations and regions away from the dominant media cluster centred around London. As the report argued:

> If we can get this sector right, not only will viewers benefit, but the future market potential for creative output from across the UK could be immense. With increasing demand for television content around the world, and new opportunities for the development of programming ideas, formats and brands across different media, the opportunities are there to be seized. (ITC, 2002b: 4)

A key finding of the review was that 90 per cent of original programme commissions come from the main terrestrial broadcasters, the BBC, ITV, Channel 4 and Channel 5. Moreover, the dominance of broadcasters in the supply chain of programmes has led to a fragility in the independent production sector. Key to this process is the fact that broadcasters capture most of the value of programmes through the control of secondary and tertiary rights. The BBC in particular had been singled out by producers for their 'boilerplate' contracts that tied them in to the BBC's commercial arm BBC Worldwide. The BBC had also been guilty, along with other broadcasters, of not reaching the 25 per cent quota established under the 1990 Broadcasting Act and annually monitored by the Office of Fair Trading. Because of fierce competition and the entrenched practices of leading broadcasters, there has historically been an overriding imbalance of power in the commissioning process (Preston, 2003).

The report recommended some key changes in the terms of trade between broadcasters and producers that would redress the imbalance of power the broadcasters had enjoyed for more than a decade. In particular, it was found that the practice of 'bundling' rights under commissioning agreements effectively 'reduces the transparency of the process and the scope for independent producers to make their own arrangements for exploitation of secondary and tertiary rights' (ITC, 2002b: 10). The issue of ownership of rights and their exploitation therefore became a key focus of state regulation of the programme-supply market and the mechanism to provide a healthy, innovative and competitive television industry. The ITC report passed on three key policy recommendations in this respect:

- clear separation of the primary rights needed by each broadcaster for its own broadcast services in the UK, from all other secondary, tertiary and international rights;

- publication by broadcasters of indicative tariffs for primary rights, so that producers are aware of the scale of funding available for such rights in the first instance;
- insisting that negotiations with distributors associated with the broadcaster are conducted separately from negotiations concerning primary rights.

(ITC, 2002b: 11)

The primary rights to television broadcasts are clearly the most valuable part of the supply chain. It is on the strength of their programmes that broadcasters survive as public-service broadcasters, advertising-driven commercial channels or niche subscription channels. However, the review also recognised the rapidly expanding market for secondary and tertiary rights. Independents through their trade organisation the Producers' Alliance for Cinema and Television (PACT) had consistently complained that broadcasters such as the BBC had either captured all the value of these rights for themselves under restrictive contracts or alternatively not bothered to exploit such rights, preventing a potential stream of revenue back to the original producer. The imbalance in the relationship was driven home by one leading production executive, Peter Bazalgette, chairman of giant international producer Endemol, who claimed that 'independent producers are like the serfs in tsarist Russia, who depended on the landowners for succour and were relatively secure at their lowly level' (Gibson, 2002). The insistence on 'holding back' any agreement on secondary and tertiary rights to see if a programme becomes a hit or not, or 'warehousing' existing assets thereby preventing programmes being licensed to secondary markets, have also been common practices among broadcasters and have arguably hindered the financial planning of independent producers. The ITC recommendations further recognised the importance of distancing the distributional arms of broadcasters from the initial commissioning process. In this way, a more competitive and fairer environment for the exploitation of secondary and tertiary rights could evolve. For example, where previous contracts would bind producers to the distributional arm of the broadcaster with the primary rights, as with the BBC and BBC Worldwide, the new regulatory regime would enable producers to seek an alternative distributor who they might consider more appropriate to reach particular international markets.

A further economic consequence of rights retention by independent producers was the ability to stabilise the finances of the company by attracting capital investment. If an independent company can retain rights, it potentially adds to the value of the company and its intangible assets (whether this be a ready-made programme or format idea). Indeed, the changing regulatory environment of independent production signalled by the ITC review triggered a series of venture-capital investments in mid-sized production companies. A report by market analysts KPMG in 2003 revealed that television and film production ranked highly as targets for venture capital across all sectors (Horsman, 2003). Although the valuation of intellectual-property rights within company assets is notoriously tricky, due to fluctuations in taste and subjective assessments of the value of programmes as brands, the move towards the retention of rights does potentially alter the financial standing of many independent production companies.

The recommendations of the ITC review of programme supply were taken largely intact to form a significant part of the Labour government's 2003 Communication Act. The Act has enforced the ITC panel's view that new terms of trade needed to be drawn up in order to redress the balance of power between broadcasters and the independent sector. To this end, the Act proposed that the new regulator Ofcom instigate and regularly enforce specific codes of practice in order to clarify the various relationships along the value chain of television production. PACT, who had lobbied both the DCMS and the ITC throughout the various reviews of programme supply and the draft Communications Bill, claimed that an important victory had been won. As Eileen Gallagher, the chairman of PACT, argued, 'Competition in markets is what brings great ideas and innovation. I think the argument that won the day with the government is that competition for ideas in television means better programmes for viewers' (Horsman, 2003).

The connection between the reward for ideas and the control of intellectual property comes through clearly in this argument. However, one consequence of the retention of rights and the pursuit of new capital investment to help grow independents from small or medium-sized enterprises into larger entities has been the pressure to consolidate market position through merger and acquisition. Exploiting a portfolio of rights through one's own distribution deals demands a certain level of economic scale. Established independent companies are put under increasing pressure to join forces through merger, and there are new concerns that instead of a diverse competitive market a new condensed sector will emerge in the post-Communications Act era.

Nevertheless, the strong lobbying by PACT to the joint committee reviewing the Communications Bill chaired by Lord Puttnam ensured the regulatory need for a more level playing field between producers and independents. The broadcasters are now duty-bound to provide a list of 'indicative tariffs' relating to the value of primary rights to enable independents to make prior decisions on the commercial viability of programmes. PACT are pursuing the issue by monitoring prices and reporting malpractice to the regulator Ofcom. Similarly, the length of the commissioning process has also been formalised, with broadcasters publishing clear guidelines to independents regarding the intervals between the submission of programme ideas, acknowledgement and initial response, the commissioning decision, the completion of contracts and the return of progress reports from producers.

Most importantly, following the ITC Review the Act ensured a defined set of primary rights to be held by the broadcaster, the duration of such rights and their renewal and guidelines to clearly separate primary-rights from secondary-rights negotiations. The codes of practice enable independents to control secondary-rights negotiations, enabling them to either maintain rights or assign rights back to the broadcaster if they so wish. One issue raised by the code in practice is the ability of independents to actually exploit secondary markets. The code does provide flexibility for producers to choose their own international distributor – a significant change from previous practice whereby broadcasters, particularly the BBC, held on to rights and exploited them through in-house international sales arms (such as BBC Worldwide). All too often, programmes with modest success were warehoused, never to see the light of day again. One final issue raised by the codes drawn up by PACT with the BBC is that of 'new media rights'. This broad-ranging right, which might include rights to control website content, interactive television content and content delivered to mobile phones, does maintain some of the inflexibility of pre-2003 contractual relations. If an independent producer, commissioned to produce a website for the BBC, were wanting to generate additional revenue through online activities, there would be grounds for further negotiations over what constitutes primary rights and secondary rights to such material based on the programme broadcast. The BBC defines such rights as 'The rights to simulcast the programme; The right to make the programme available on demand; The use of extracts of the programme on any web-sites associated with the programme and the use of extracts of the programme on any generic sites' (PACT, 2004). Given the burgeoning opportunities for the commercial exploitation of such rights, it would appear that the BBC has retained some of its omnipresent control of the rights to license funded broadcast material to the exclusion of commercial new-media enterprises.

The rise and rise of television formats

If there is one area of television that has transformed the international market for programmes since the 1990s it has been television formats. The principle of formats is simple: have a programme idea, write it up as a treatment, claim copyright in it and license the underlying format to as many countries as possible. Formats are not new; many of television history's leading quiz shows had their origins in the USA, such as *The Price is Right* or *Wheel of Fortune*. But the latest wave of formats has increased the proportion of global television that originates from licensed programming. For example, one of the most successful formats of the late 1990s and the early twenty-first century was the Celador production *Who Wants to be a Millionaire?* The programme first aired in the UK on ITV in 1998, and a US version soon topped the ratings on the ABC network the following year. The format was subsequently licensed to more than forty territories and screened in over sixty-five countries worldwide. The reason why formats are attractive to broadcasters is also self-evident. Knowing that the programme which a broadcaster is funding is already a hit in other territories is a major attraction. Buying licences to successful formats saves time and resources on researching and innovating new programme ideas. Formats reduce risk. Although the ubiquitous rise of formats may appear to be producing a global homogenisation of television programming, quite often they are tailored to the needs of local markets. This 'reversioning' of television formats to heterogeneous cultural tastes has been the hallmark of many hit programmes. One of the most successful formats in this respect has been Endemol's 'reality television' programme *Big Brother*.

Endemol Entertainment is the largest producer of independent television productions in Europe. Its roots are in the Netherlands, established in 1994 by two television producers, Joop van den Ende and John de Mol. The company's key strategy has been to claim a stake in leading production companies across Europe to help roll out its catalogue of television formats across the continent. This strategy has expanded further into other regions of the world, including the USA. Aside from being a production base of independent content, the company also operated as a distributor. However, in 2000 the company was sold to the Spanish telecoms group Telefonica. The new alliance places Endemol as the basic content producer for the Spanish company's global operations in broadcasting, the Internet, third-generation mobile phones and other platforms. Rather than vertically integrate its development, production, distribution and exhibition of media content, Telefonica has outsourced content production to one of the leading specialists in the market. Endemol has streamlined its activities by selling its distribution division to concentrate on production of programmes rather than handle third-party content.

Big Brother was by far and away its most successful exploitation of television formats. The format for the programme builds on three cornerstones of contemporary television: realism through hidden cameras; interactivity through viewer participation in weekly evictions via digital television, telephony or the Internet; and the veneration of the contestants as 'new' celebrities. The programme that places ten strangers in a prefabricated house under twenty-four-hour surveillance has built a cult following in all the countries where it has been produced. Interestingly, each version of the programme has been produced by an independent production company with corporate affiliation to Endemol and is primarily aired on channels that have a minority share in a particular national market. *Big Brother* aims to boost ratings as a summer-long media event and has proved very successful at capturing audiences at a time of the year usually associated with a drop in television viewing. In the UK, the programme has at times tripled the average audience share of Channel 4, and the fifth series ended with the second highest rating ever for Channel 4 (ranking just below the audience for the final episode of *Friends*), with nine million viewers tuning in to see the winner. A further innovation in the format has been the incorporation of interactive elements over the Internet and via mobile phones. Again, websites have been produced in alliance with local Internet companies rather than through Endemol's own new-media platform Endemol.com. Sponsorship by mobile-phone companies such as O_2 in 2002 and Talk Talk in 2004 have also helped to generate mutual benefits for service providers and the producers of the programme. Voting via SMS text messages raised more than £1.35m in revenue in 2002 (*The Economist*, 2002), and in 2004 additional revenue was raised through the sale of *Big Brother* ringtones, wallpaper and text alerts.

The original series in the Netherlands created international news coverage after occupants of the *Big Brother* house had sex on television. In the 1998–9 financial year, the programme helped boost the company's turnover by nearly 25 per cent, and the programme itself has generated huge advertising revenues for the various broadcasters that have commissioned *Big Brother*. On nearly all of the channels on which the programme has been broadcast, the viewing figures have boosted what were otherwise modest market shares. Endemol's strategy of developing original content and selling its rights on to broadcasters through strategic alliances with domestic production companies has proven a winning formula for global production. However, breaking the American market has still proven problematic. The US version of *Big Brother* teamed up Endemol, CBS and AOL to deliver the fourth version of the format (after the Netherlands, Germany and Spain). After successfully establishing partnerships with both a prestigious broadcaster and an Internet company, the programme failed to capture the imagination of US audiences as it had in Europe. To this end, the failure of the European format in the USA highlights the continued parochial focus of American media tastes.

Big Brother and other formats like it reveal the importance of protecting original ideas. Indeed, when the *Big Brother* format took off in 1999, the programme makers had to fight off a legal challenge from the makers of another 'reality television' programme, *Survivor*, who claimed that Endemol had stolen the underlying idea of the format where ten people are isolated from the rest of the world and gradually eliminated one by one until there is a winner. The owners of *Survivor* failed in their attempt to convince a judge that copyright in the format had been breached mainly because there were enough differences in the two programmes to distance *Big Brother* from its rival. Nevertheless, there have been instances of re-versioning format ideas in some parts of the world that copy US or British formats without a licence. For every successful format, there are probably half a dozen programmes that clone the idea with a slight twist. Policing formats and ensuring that their intellectual property can be enforced are now important aspects of the global trade in television programmes. As one independent producer, David Brook of the Optimistic Network, has outlined, 'with copyright of TV formats something of a grey area, there is frankly no better way to protect a great idea than to make it' (Brook, 2004).

Conclusion

The majority of the UK's 600 or more independent companies are risk-averse and would not have the financial strength or commercial wherewithal to build international distribution arms to expand their commercial activities (Preston, 2002). Most producers are too busy with the day-to-day activities of making programmes and running a tight ship. Nevertheless, the recent legislative changes under the Communications Act 2003 do provide infrastructural support in terms of a set code of practice in the commissioning process with each broadcaster, and clearly defined boundaries of rights ownership and exploitation. The arm's-length approach between the ownership of primary rights by broadcasters and the exploitation of secondary and tertiary rights by independent producers may have some significant effects on the structure of the UK and possibly the global television market. The fact that it has taken legislative intervention to create the climate for such change should not be forgotten. For what the interventionist policy has recognised is that, in order for a variety of creative talent to function in the global and highly concentrated world of television broadcasting, some power in the balance of rights ownership has to be ceded back to the original creators of content. Power in this context means choice to make strategic decisions on what a producer thinks is the best way forward for a particular product. Throughout the commissioning process of the 1990s, the balance in the UK context had severely restricted the opportunities for small to medium-sized production companies to expand, take risks, innovate programming and flourish commercially. The outcome of the 2003 Act might be the potential for asset-led television producers to boost the local cultural economy through investment in talent, leading to the research and development of new ideas.

There is a caveat to this version of the creative boom in independent television production. There are already signs that the independent production sector is bulking up its capacity to compete on the UK and international stage through merger and acquisition. I have already mentioned the rapid expansionist policy of pre-school producer Hit Entertainment, but economies of scale and scope are being sought across other genres too. This process is not unfamiliar in the media industries in general, and it is mainly driven by the centrality of leveraging economic value from intellectual-property rights that dictate the way in which creative and marketing energies are pumped into a few winners, with many losers hitting the cutting-room floor. In terms of the expansionist march of television markets in the digital era, with thousands of hours of programming to fill, this process is in its infancy, and only time will tell how the balance of power between the established 'big fish' of broadcasting and the emerging pool of small, varied and creative producers eventually pans out.

Study question

How has the Communications Act 2003 affected the balance of rights between broadcasters and independent producers? What is likely to happen to the industry under these new terms of trade?

Further reading

Howkins, J. (2001), *The Creative Economy: How People Make Money from Ideas*, London: Penguin Books.
Viljoen, D. (2003), *The Art of the Deal: Essential Guide to Business Affairs for Television and Film Producers*, 2nd edn, London: PACT Publications.

Relevant websites

Producers' Alliance for Cinema and Television – http://www.pact.co.uk/
British Television Distributors' Association – http://www.btda.org/

7 Celebrity and image rights

Introduction

A film director tries to prevent a major international media conglomerate from rebranding a cable television station using his adopted name. A pop star prepares to do battle with a football club over the ownership of a nickname that its fans have been using for more than seventy years. A long-retired athlete makes a complaint to Ofcom and then threatens to sue a telecoms company for parodying his likeness from the 1970s in a highly successful advertising campaign. An ageing rock star threatens to take out an injunction to prevent a music journalist with the same name from writing a column in an American journal. Welcome to the crazy world of 'image rights' and a power struggle waged by celebrities to control all forms of publicity associated with their name and likeness.

In this chapter, we shall discover the inroads into media rights that have been made by, or on behalf of, leading entertainers and sports stars. As we have seen in other areas of media activity, the concept of image rights opens up wider philosophical questions around intellectual property that have a direct impact on the political economy of the media.

The cult of celebrity takes up increasing amounts of media output, and it is not difficult to see why stars and their agents seek to control this particular aspect of their 'brand' value. As Lane (1999: 48) notes, 'celebrity seems to exert a disproportionate influence on the Zeitgeist', and in 'this merchandising melee, traders and celebrity are left squabbling over entitlement to the financial spoils' (Lane, 1999: 49). However, as we shall discover, in spite of the concept of image rights gaining purchase within the entertainment industries, there is no legislation that recognises a statutory right of an individual to control the commercial use of their image.

So what are the key legal and philosophical arguments for a property right in a person's image? Image rights refer to the commercial use of someone's image, voice, likeness, name or signature. They have become a common trait of the contemporary media economy and are strongly protected and policed by leading celebrities and their agents. Historically, there has been a general suspicion within UK courts about recognising specific rights of publicity for individuals and the claim that a celebrity's image or likeness may have been misappropriated. English courts have resisted such claims due to the belief that property in a person is 'a commodification too far' (Cornish, 1999: 31). Much of this chapter deals with the ways in which existing intellectual-property laws have been used to protect celebrity images, often stretching the boundaries of the law in new and innovative ways. The rewards are great, and the ability for stars to control the use and commercial value of their names and images is paramount in the often fleeting career enjoyed by many celebrities. Exploiting fame and notoriety is therefore the 'name of the game', and the protection of image rights has become one of the hottest topics for media and entertainment lawyers. As Drahos and Braithwaite (2002) point out, stardom operates in a hierarchy of fame from the local to the global, where only a minority reach the status of a megastar. As they suggest, 'a world in which everyone is a superstar is a world in which no one is' (Drahos and Braithwaite, 2002: 179).

The philosophy of image rights

The merchandising and endorsement of celebrities is now commonplace and forms a central component of the media industry. As in any form of commerce, celebrities seek to protect their commercial value through various legal mechanisms. Legal protection is sought in the belief that individuals have legitimate proprietary rights in their own person and any use of its image, signature or even style. Whether or not celebrities should be afforded image rights centres on a range of arguments drawn from the political philosophy of property. As we have discovered throughout the book, intellectual property refers to the abstract notion that individuals should have proprietary rights over the creations of their mind. We have learnt that intellectual property is justified in various ways depending on the philosophical point of view. Therefore, one might want to justify intellectual property in an individual's persona under the Lockean principle of natural rights. Here, celebrities may claim natural proprietary rights over their image created out of the labour involved in becoming famous in the first instance. The natural right to own one's image is born of the belief that, after years of effort to achieve fame and notoriety, individuals who achieve celebrity status have accumulated enough significance for their identity to be recognised as publicly valuable and commercially marketable. Just as a tangible piece of property can increase in value by home improvements, so the reasoning goes, a celebrity's worth as intangible property comes from their efforts to become 'somebody' from being a 'nobody'.

But recourse to natural-rights arguments throws up some awkward questions when attempting to clarify where a person's fame originates. Celebrity, the recognition of an individual in the public domain, is not necessarily the direct result of a person's labour. There are many other factors which create stars, most notably the media and its veneration and celebration of an individual. As Beverley-Smith (2002: 295) argues, 'In most cases, fame – and the opportunities for its exploitation – does not derive directly from the actual process of labouring or from the performance of particular tasks'. Indeed, the celebrity images that pervade our contemporary media are part of wider social and cultural processes that represent the focal point of diverse cultural practices and desires. As Rosemary Coombe (1992: 2) points out, celebrity names and images

> are not simply marks of identity or simple commodities; they are also cultural texts – floating signifiers that are continually invested with libidinal energies, social longings, and [. . .] political aspirations. The names and likenesses of the famous are constitutive of our cultural heritage and resonate with meanings that exceed the intentions or the interests of those they identify or resemble.

Similar sentiments have been voiced by Madow (1993: 2), who also asks whether the law 'should confer a source of additional wealth on athletes and entertainers who are already very handsomely compensated [. . .]?' The 'sweat of the brow' thesis collapses on several fronts if we understand the way in which celebrity culture works and the symbiotic role played by the media and the audience that venerate them. Celebrities rely upon an entourage of agents, publicists and entertainment lawyers to support their relationships with advertisers, sponsors, merchandise licensees and assorted media outlets. The necessity to employ such intermediaries is enough to signify that the activity of entertainers is not the sole driver of the star economy. Rather, it is a whole set of contractual negotiations premised on a perceived value of an individual and their symbolic capital in wider public life.

Alternative arguments do exist to justify the protection of image rights. It could be argued that stars are motivated to become famous in the knowledge that proprietary ownership of their image enables them to exploit their commercial value and accumulate wealth. This utilitarian approach to image rights lays emphasis on the ability of proprietary rights to operate as an incentive to innovation and creative production. The main problem here is that the lack of a proprietary right in someone's personality, as is the case in the UK, does not in itself impair the ability of stars to exploit their name and image through endorsements or any other commercial activity. Such rights are simply not needed for stars to cash in on their fame.

The utilitarian argument also throws up a second possibility for justifying image rights. Restricted rights to celebrity images would ensure economic efficiency in the market for celebrity merchandise and endorsements. A monopoly right to the commercial use of a celebrity name or image would maximise its economic worth by restricted access. In this scenario, an exclusive right to a particular image of a star would push up its value to an optimum price. Much like an auction for a rare signature, the right to own a person's image right would go to the highest bidder. However, the market-efficiency model is also problematic when faced with the broader cultural context of fame. Maximising economic value does not always equate with the wider cultural value of celebrity and notoriety. If images are given away for free or at a marginal cost, the coverage of the celebrity is far more likely to be widespread and ubiquitous, therefore more publicly noticeable, conspicuous, and needless to say famous. In some instances, winning mass appeal arguably has more potential economic value than exclusively sold proprietary image rights.

The application of mainstream ideas on intellectual property rights to the appropriation of a star's image rights are fraught with contradictions. There are broader political questions to be asked regarding any claim to monopolise commercial rights in this way. Critiques of the 'right of publicity' in the USA point to wider issues of censorship through the control of publicity rights and ask whether intellectual property law is the right mechanism to confer even more wealth on those who enjoy handsome remuneration for the work they already do as pop stars, actors or sportsmen (Madow, 1993: 2). As we shall see in our case study of sports image rights, it is not always clear that a proprietary right to an individual's image, name or likeness is the most effective way of protecting their economic and broader cultural interests. Nevertheless, as Beverley-Smith (2002: 315) points out,

> At the broadest level, claims for property rights in personality are but one manifestation of the proprietarian creed, which some see as increasingly pervasive in intellectual property law, whereby property rights have a moral priority over other rights and interests, and activities that first give rise to economic value also necessarily create property rights. Property rights trump the wider community interests, and everything is capable of private ownership.

This argument seems particularly apt in the context of celebrities and their image rights. The increased privatisation of star images, allied to a general process of intensified commodification of culture, removes from the debate broader issues pertinent to understanding contemporary culture, such as how the media and entertainment industries are structured as aggregated industries and who they are for.

Trademarking an individual

Trademark law has been reluctant to provide monopoly rights to personalities. Classically, trademarks require that the indicia in question be recognisably distinct and be capable of registration as a trademark in relation to certain goods and services. In this way, trademarks act as a 'badge of origin' which may, for a sports star for example, prove to be a very important marketing tool to ensure both reputation and financial reward. They also prevent others from exploiting the good name of a celebrity without permission. However, it is arguable that a person's name does not necessarily carry such distinctiveness, as many people may share the same name. For example, in 2002, the former Rolling Stones member Bill Wyman attempted to prevent a music journalist with the same name from writing his column, claiming that readers would mistakenly believe that the articles were written by the former guitarist. The rock star, who had registered his name as a trademark, requested that the Atlanta journalist post a disclaimer on everything he wrote indicating that he was not Bill Wyman of the Rolling Stones. The threatened lawsuit was soon dropped when it was apparent that the journalist had been called Bill Wyman from birth in 1961, which predated the rock star changing his name to Wyman by deed poll in 1964 (BBC, 2002). The case illustrates that names are descriptive indicators and do not automatically function as a mark of origin to certain goods and services. However, the Wyman example is the tip of an ever-expanding list of legal challenges to control celebrity names and images as the economic stakes of celebrity and fame have dramatically increased.

So in what ways have celebrities turned to trademarks to protect their image, and why is this increasingly acceptable? There have been well-publicised cases where third-party use of a trademark without permission has not been viewed as an infringement by the courts. For example, in a case involving the legal estate of Elvis Presley, the name Elvis was not deemed to be distinctive enough to function as a 'badge of origin'. Buying a piece of memorabilia with the image of Elvis on it did not instantly suggest to the consumer that the source of the product was the Elvis estate (Lane, 2002). Case law had only contemplated damage where there was some common connection in the business activity of the two parties.

Quite often, monopoly rights in a celebrity image or name cannot be given due to their very popularity in the media and general ubiquitous coverage. The death of Diana, Princess of Wales, in 1997 led to the rise of new commercial enterprises eager to capitalise on her global popularity and fame by exploiting her name and image in a wide array of merchandise. Many of these uses were challenged by the Princess of Wales Memorial Fund as a form of false endorsement. In an attempt to protect the image and signature of the late Princess, the Trust made numerous applications to register Diana as a trademark. The problem for the Trust came in the fact that during her lifetime Diana was the most photographed woman in world. The Patent Office turned down applications to trademark Diana's image because any image of the Princess would not necessarily lead people to believe that the use of her image would act as a 'badge of origin', as it was so ubiquitous. Several challenges to the use of Diana's name also failed because it failed to perform the source-designating function that trademarks require.

This gap in UK legislation contrasts with the United States and with European territories where various personality rights are protected. In the USA, the Right to Publicity under the Constitution provides any citizen with the right to control how their identity is used commercially. Crucial in the evolution of the publicity right was the 1953 case involving rival bubblegum manufacturers Haelean Laboratories, Inc. and Topps Chewing Gum, Inc., who were battling to gain the rights to print images of leading major-league baseball players on their 'trading cards'. The Haelean case established that individuals 'possessed a property right in their own images' and that 'this right could be transferred to a third party' to enforce rights from unauthorised use (Hylton, 2001: 274). However, there remain difficulties in attempts to protect celebrity names, and there continue to be battlegrounds over the use of certain names and their various uses. For example, in the US context, some celebrities have failed to corral all uses of their names even where they make a claim to longstanding registration of trademarks. In June 2003, the New York film director Spike Lee took an injunction out against cable channel Spike TV over the infringement of trademark and damages to his 'right of publicity'. Spike TV, a niche channel aimed at young men focusing on cars, technology, sports and other generic 'men's things', was a rebranded name for Viacom-owned cable channel TNN. Lee claimed that the channel was seeking to exploit his name to attract customers who associated the word Spike with his own 'hip' and 'cool' persona fostered by his films and advertising activities.

Although the president of TNN admitted that Lee had been one of the reasons to associate the word Spike with the rebranded station, he also pointed out that there were many other famous spikes, and its use also had strong associations with basketball and baseball that men would be familiar with. The injunction caused Viacom to pull the promotional campaign for the channel to the extent that TNN simply became known as the 'New TNN' for the term of the litigation. However, the court requested Lee to put $2.5m bond on the case before moving to trial. The significance of the potential losses and the immediate backlash against Lee in the US media probably led to the litigation being halted, effectively leaving Viacom home free. The case illustrates the potential power handed over to celebrities by the legal protection of image rights. That an individual could consider challenging the use of a common word such as 'spike' reveals the measure of power over the production of meaning which such proprietary rights deliver. Moreover, it delimits the 'expressive and communicative opportunities' afforded others in the creative commons (Madow, 1993: 7).

'Passing off' and sports-star endorsement

Sports stars have increasingly used the media to control the representation of their image. Managing their public perception demands a constant vigil to police the use of images and any suggestion that a sports star is making an endorsement of a product or service. Such controlled access invariably comes at a high cost for the advertiser or publication concerned. When a sports star's image is illegitimately used, various legal remedies have been drawn upon to remunerate lack of consent and any resulting injury (financial or to goodwill). In the UK, case law is just beginning to side in favour of sports celebrities and their commercial rights. The legal representatives of sports stars are turning to innovative interpretations of law to protect celebrity names and likenesses. These include damages brought against goodwill and misrepresentation under the common-law tort of 'passing off', which has been used in court cases where well-known personalities have complained against the illegitimate use of their image.

The sports-celebrity industry has gained significant encouragement from recent cases involving proprietary rights in sport. In March 2002, the High Court decision in the case of *Eddie Irvine v. Talksport* effectively recognised the value of sports image rights and conferred protection on them. Talksport had used a doctored photograph of the racing driver in a promotional leaflet that the commercial radio station had circulated to media buyers and potential advertisers. Fewer than 1,000 leaflets had been distributed; but the business-affairs director for the Formula One team Jordan, Ian Philips, had noticed the driver's inclusion in the promotion and alerted him to the fact. Talksport had digitally manipulated Irvine's image in a photograph of him holding a mobile phone, replacing the phone by a portable radio carrying the logo of Talk Radio. Irvine's legal representatives argued that the leaflet was suggestive of an endorsement of Talksport by the driver.

The law of passing off attempts to protect the goodwill in an unregistered trademark. The case centred on whether or not a famous sports celebrity had acquired a valuable reputation and if the goodwill in the star's name or likeness had been misrepresented to the market as being licensed by the individual concerned. Mr Justice Laddie held that the manipulation of the image for commercial gain clearly represented false endorsement. Irvine's value as a brand was viewed as being affected, causing damage to his goodwill, reputation and name. Mr Justice Laddie's ruling confirmed that the name and image of a sports star can be constitutive of a brand, with all the various economic rights associated with that status. Importantly, it also confirmed that 'passing off' cases involving sports stars no longer rested on the two parties sharing a common field of commercial activity. This was a significant leap in the potential breadth of protection afforded by the courts to celebrity endorsements. Mr Justice Laddie concluded:

> Even without the evidence given at the trial of this action, the court can take judicial notice of the fact that it is common for famous people to exploit their names and images by way of endorsement. They do it not only in their own field of expertise but, depending on the extent of their fame and notoriety, in a wider field also ... Manufacturers and retailers recognise the realities of the marketplace when they pay for well-known personalities to endorse their goods. The law of passing off should do likewise. (cited in Boyd, 2003)

The ruling went short of providing a complete monopoly right over star images, particularly with reference to character merchandising; but nevertheless the Irvine ruling has encouraged sports stars to believe that the courts will protect their commercial interests when their images and likenesses are illegitimately used.

A second, and related, instance of false endorsement occurred when the former long-distance runner David Bedford challenged the telephone directory service The Number for using a caricature of his persona in their nationwide marketing campaign. The deregulation of telephone directory services in August 2003 had led to a new competitive market for such services previously monopolised by BT. One new entrant, the operator The Number, owned by the US call-centre company InfoNXX, runs the distinctive 118 118 enquiry service. The service made a major impact on the market in a £70 million cross-media advertising campaign that used a comic theme starring two long-distance runners wearing retro-1970s running vests with two hoops, red socks and pale blue shorts. The characters also had distinctive drooping moustaches and long straggly hair. The ads soon gained a cult following and were critically acclaimed for their humour and innovation. The campaign also appeared to be incredibly successful, as the 118 118 service mopped up 50 per cent of the directory service market in the opening months of operation (Oliver, 2003). However, as the advertising campaign gained recognition among audiences and plaudits from the advertising industry, Bedford, long retired from athletics and now the race director of the London Marathon, approached lawyers to question whether his image had been misrepresented and illegitimately used for commercial ends.

Bedford made a claim to assert his image rights as the campaign for 118 118 began to gain momentum. In January 2004, Bedford won an important victory when the newly formed media regulator Ofcom upheld a ruling that the ad campaign had used a caricature of Bedford which was a breach of Rule 6.5 of the Advertising Standards Code that protects the privacy and exploitation of the individual. The regulator found that the campaign used a 'comically exaggerated representation' of Bedford that was considered against the Code's stipulation that 'living people must not be portrayed, caricatured or referred to in advertisements without their permission' (Ofcom, 2004). However, in spite of recognising that The Number 'neither sought nor obtained David Bedford's permission to be caricatured', the regulator decided that the former runner had not suffered any damages to his reputation or 'actual financial harm'. Given the amount of money that The Number had spent on the campaign, Ofcom ruled that to ban the campaign would be disproportionate to the money already invested by the directory service. The ruling gave a fillip to Bedford's claim that he had not endorsed the campaign but also took any potential sting out of potential civil action regarding loss of commercial revenue from image-rights endorsement. Bedford had reportedly estimated damages of £250,000 (Pearce, 2004) based on the ruling in favour of Eddie Irvine and an out-of-court settlement by Ian Botham.

Problems with passing-off claims

Bedford's case is indicative of the mounting pressure for legislative recognition of image rights and the proactive stance taken by sports stars (even those who have long since faded from the public domain) to control and assert such rights. However, there does appear to be a divergence in the regulations governing the use of sports celebrity images in advertising and endorsements. Under the Advertising Standards Code, Ofcom clearly gave notice that the use of the former athlete's likeness should have been sanctioned by Bedford before transmission. However, Ofcom did not have the power to order damages, nor did it deem The Number's actions to be punishable by a fine. This decision runs contrary to the judgement in the Irvine case that gave £25,000 in damages after appeal as the amount of money the racing driver would have expected to receive had he endorsed the Talksport campaign. The Irvine case largely rested on the damage to goodwill and reputation of a sports star who was well known and whom the public might have expected to endorse such products and services in question. However, as Pearce (2004) points out, Bedford was an individual who had fleeting success in the early 1970s and whose reputation as a 'celebrity' was virtually insignificant. If anything, the 118 118 campaign had the positive effect of raising awareness of the former athlete, putting him back in the public eye after thirty years of obscurity.

An important aspect of passing-off cases is the issue of false endorsement. In both the Botham and Bedford cases, it is debatable whether the audience would believe that the Guinness and 118 118 ads were commercially connected with either sportsman. In the case of Botham, Guinness would have bought archive material which most people would recognise as being such. They would not necessarily expect the use of such historical images to be endorsed by the star himself. Unlike the manipulation of the Irvine image by Talksport, Guinness merely used the image of Botham from the 1981 Ashes series as a backdrop to its main message. Similarly, with Bedford, the campaign used comic caricatures performed by actors in a parody of a 1970s athlete. While it was dishonest of The Number to claim that the caricatures were not based on Bedford but rather a 'generic 1970s athlete', including the US runner Steve Prefontaine, it also stretched the bounds of credibility to suggest that the public would expect Bedford to have implicitly endorsed such a campaign. There was no specific reference that Bedford had endorsed the campaign which would have broken the Advertising Standards Code, and Bedford was not known for endorsing products and would not have the same commercial value as a contemporary sports celebrity.

Protection via the back door: connections with privacy

As we have noted, the notoriety and fame that come with celebrity status are a double-edged sword. The media are the important conduit for the public to be informed and learn about individuals and their celebrity lives. This means that stars must court publicity in order to maintain their public profile and build their reputations. However, publicity is often of a negative nature; and the media, in particular the populist tabloid press, are as quick to cut a celebrity down once in their prime as to build them up as extraordinary human beings. The management of image and reputation therefore becomes a central facet of a celebrity's public-relations efforts. In extreme cases, stars will turn to the law for protection. The classic remedy for ill-judged or untruthful statements in the media has been the law of defamation or libel, and many celebrities have been successful in gaining damages after the event. However, a potentially stronger control is emerging through the application of the European Convention on Human Rights that attempts to balance the individual's right to privacy and the media's freedom of expression. Several high-profile cases have emerged in the UK that have interpreted the Human Rights Act 1998 in new ways to provide protectionist remedies for celebrities in their attempt to censure media coverage and illicit use of potentially damaging images to their reputations and goodwill. Privacy law is the flipside of rights in personality.

In the Naomi Campbell case against the *Daily Mirror*, the 'supermodel' claimed a breach of confidence after the paper had published an article on her attendance at a drug rehabilitation centre run by Narcotics Anonymous in February 2001. Campbell claimed that the article, which used photographs of the model leaving the centre and laid emphasis on her drug addiction, broke her confidence with the drug rehabilitation agency and ultimately caused an invasion of privacy. The case was heard in the High Court (where Campbell initially won damages of £3,500), the Court of Appeal (where the *Mirror* won its appeal and Campbell was asked to cover the *Mirror*'s costs) and the House of Lords (where a majority vote by five law lords of 3:2 overturned the Court of Appeal's ruling and upheld Campbell's right of privacy).

A similar use of human-rights legislation and breach of confidence was raised in the case involving Catherine Zeta Jones and Michael Douglas in their suit against *Hello!* magazine. The celebrity couple had sold exclusive rights of access to their wedding to the celebrity magazine *OK!* and had the guests at their New York wedding in November 2000 sign confidentiality agreements not to release any photographs of the wedding to the public. Excluded from the wedding, rivals *Hello!* obtained illicit photographs of the wedding and rushed to publish them as a 'spoiler' before the 'official' photographs appeared in *OK!*. Zeta Jones and Douglas sued the magazine on the grounds of breach of privacy under laws protecting commercial confidentiality. The High Court ruled in their favour due to the fact that the breach of confidentiality involved the commercial use of the intrusive photographs. *Hello!* were ordered to pay damages of £1m to *OK!* magazine and to pay three-quarters of the actors' legal fees. The ruling introduced a new level of protection afforded to celebrities who enter into exclusive commercial contracts with the media regarding licensing rights of access and publication. Nevertheless, *Hello!* magazine continued to make the argument that the practice of 'spoiling' such deals was part and parcel of the celebrity-magazine business and that Mr Justice Lindsay's interpretation of the law had compromised the freedom of the press to report on issues of high public interest.

Conclusion

In spite of all this legal manoeuvring to protect the commercial worth of celebrities, the term 'image rights' still elicits confusion as to what they are and who is set to benefit. There remains an important distinction between the use of a celebrity to endorse a product or service and the use of a celebrity image to merchandise a product. As the Irvine case shows, under the common-law tort of passing off, the UK courts now seem prepared to recognise the commercial rights of celebrities to be associated with the marketing of products. But attempts to monopolise image rights or rights of publicity have not found favour in the courts or in UK legislation.

A further distinction to be made is the difference between proprietary rights, such as trademarks in a celebrity's name or signature associated with specific goods and services, and contractual rights that pertain to commercial relationships between two or more parties. For instance, the football industry has introduced standard-form agreements between clubs and players that include certain contractual obligations on both sides to remunerate players for commercial and media activities undertaken outside of their playing duties. The 'image-rights clause' is a contractual agreement and not based on the assignment of any proprietary rights that a player might hold.

The paradox for contemporary celebrities is that, as they attempt to commercially control the use of their name and image, the number of media outlets for their exposure is rapidly expanding to almost uncontrollable proportions. More broadly, legal critics such as Lawrence Lessig (2001) have argued that by attempts to enclose new forms of intellectual property, such as image rights, innovations in new media are potentially being undermined.

A further issue raised by the enclosure of image rights is that it potentially stifles the effective reporting of celebrities and wider aspects of popular culture. The encroachment of privacy laws into the control of commercial images of celebrities suggests that the freedom of the press is under threat. Attempts to monopolise names and images raise questions of balance between privacy and press freedom. While celebrities enjoy the often well-earned rewards of their various talents and enterprise, arguably it should not be at the expense of the exposure of disreputable behaviour or the general reportage of their activities that increasingly capture the imagination of large sections of the general public.

Study question

What is the difference between a proprietary right and a contractual right in someone's image? Discuss ways in which famous celebrities use intellectual-property rights to control or manipulate their media coverage.

Further reading

Beverley-Smith, H. (2002), *The Commercial Appropriation of Personality*, Cambridge: Cambridge University Press.

Relevant websites

UK Trademarks Register – http://www.patent.gov.uk/tm/dbase/common/down.htm
Couchman/Harrington Associates – http://www.chass.co.uk/
Trademark Blog – http://trademark.blog.us/blog/

8 Intellectual property and the internet

> For information age entrepreneurs [...] the protection of property is the *sine qua non* of successful activities.
>
> (Christopher May, 2002: 131)

Introduction: Internet redux

When the Internet truly took off as a mass medium in 1996 in the guise of the World Wide Web, it was like an untamed wilderness ripe for discovery, and new users marvelled at the wondrous and instantaneous way in which information and images could be pulled to their desktops from around the world. It was an uncharted digital landscape with endless potential and possibilities. In 2005, a mere nine years later, our perception of the web is somewhat different. The first wave of e-commerce has come and gone, and lessons have been learnt. The survivors of the dot.com boom and bust of the early millennium – Amazon, Google, Yahoo, e-Bay – are now the doyens of the web, drawing strength from their global customer base and the ubiquitousness of their brands. More and more of us are happy to immerse ourselves in the virtual worlds of the Internet and to browse, buy and bank online. But perhaps most importantly in the context of media rights, more and more of what we do online and the ways in which the online world is organised are sanctioned by licence agreements, registration and contracts all protected under the sign of intellectual-property law. The analogy of the Internet as a wide-open frontier offering a brave new world is a common one, but so too is the belief that huge tracts of this virtual world are being fenced off for exclusive use available at a price. James Boyle makes the outcome of this blatantly clear when he says: 'Think of barbed wire. Ranchers want to use barbed wire to protect their herds, but the wire will enclose not only their lands but also portions of the commons' (Boyle, 2000b: 2,020).

As we discovered in Chapter 3, new legislation prompted by the corporate interests of the media industry, supported by the international treaties under multilateral trade negotiations such as WIPO and TRIPS and finally enacted through the DMCA and the European Copyright Directive, is precisely an outcome of this type of thinking – that marshalling access and preventing leakiness from the digital environment will prove both economically and, it is argued, culturally beneficial. Key to this process of enclosure is the ability to govern the use of this new territory. How we engage and interact with the Internet – usually via a web browser that inevitably comes ready packed with the operating system on our PCs or Apple Macs – is increasingly guided within certain parameters, many of which we might remain blissfully unaware of. Antitrust battles between the US competition authorities and the giant software company Microsoft from 2000 to 2002 were not purely about abuse of market power and monopoly. They were also about the ability of one company to set the default mode of access and use of media applications (the Windows Media Player) across the web and on people's desktops. In the USA, Microsoft got off with what amounted to a slapped wrist; and, even when the EU's competition directorate took issue with its monopolistic practices centred around the bundling of applications with its Windows operating system (levying 1 per cent of gross revenues), the company remained omnipresent in the software market. New threats to freedom and innovation are continuing to occur, and many of them are associated with intellectual property and corporate power to influence governments to implement the necessary legislation and coerce consumer behaviour.

In this chapter, we shall return to some of the themes raised in Chapter 3 regarding digital media but also look more specifically at how media rights shape the ways in which the Internet is developing and the ways in which it can be used. The seemingly inseparable couplet of the Internet and copyright has made headlines for nearly a decade, with Napster and file-sharing more generally most often cited as public enemy number one. Copyright remains important, but in this review of the Internet we shall also look at issues of trademark and patents. But first, it is worth reminding ourselves exactly where the Internet came from and how its very fabric is born of an open, shared ethic to enable users to distribute and access information freely, largely unrestrained from intellectual-property concerns. I do not want to repeat the many other histories of the Internet now available (John Naughton's *A Brief History of the Future* (1999) is as good a place as any to start), but want us merely to remind ourselves what the driving motivation for developing it was, what principles drove its construction and where intellectual-property rights fit into our understanding of this process.

The 'neutral' network

A fledgling Internet began to emerge in the 1960s. It arose out of a desire to provide a common architecture to connect independent computing systems, initially for the US military and soon afterwards for civilian use mainly by research universities. A handful of universities in the USA had developed internal computing networks that enabled multiple computers to be connected to each other. ARPANET was the first consolidated effort to bridge this system into a network of networks. The simple idea was to allow any computer in the network to access data held on another, no matter how far apart the two end points were. This end-to-end network formed the basis of an emerging standard, a common network architecture that was built on co-operation and shared knowledge in a genuine effort to find interoperability and efficient means of pooling information. The philosophy of the early pioneers of the information age – often evoking association with the libertarian values of hippies and geeks – has endured in the shape of the open source movement and peer-to-peer practices. A number of important standard protocols were established throughout the 1970s and 1980s, such as File Transfer Protocol (FTP), Telnet, Internet Protocol (IP) and Transport Control Protocol (TCP), that enabled files to be moved across the network with relative ease.

In the context of intellectual-property rights, nobody owned the source code to these applications. In this sense, the backbone of the Internet was a public resource, open to anyone with the technical means and know-how. The collaborative origins of this process also untied the writing of code from the notion of the romantic author. Creativity and innovation were born from shared information, building upon what others had done, not for private gain, with no particular individual laying claim to authorship. The romantic author did not exist in this new era of information. As Lessig (2001) writes, the origins of the Internet also owe much to the altruistic behaviour of large corporations and the US government. The neutral network that the Internet ran on – what Lessig terms the 'physical layer' of wires and switches – was actually owned and run by AT&T, the state-sanctioned monopoly on telecoms. Given the increasing corporate stranglehold on the Internet, there is clearly some irony here. AT&T's opening up of the telecommunications spectrum for the early Internet to run on is vitally important for the 'neutrality' of the network. It means anyone can join it, adapt it and use it for their own purposes. It does not mean they do not have to pay for the privilege of accessing the wires – for the network has to be owned and maintained by someone – but the use of these wires is not controlled.

The neutral network proved even more important as the Internet evolved into its most revolutionary state, the World Wide Web. The web emerged as a practical solution to an ongoing problem. In spite of the fact that computers could exchange information via the Internet, all too often the data were stored on incompatible databases and limited the ability of one network to 'talk' to another. The solution came from a physics researcher, Tim Berners-Lee. He attempted to standardise the network by bringing together certain protocols from the Internet, such as FTP, IP/TCP and an innovative new language, Hypertext Mark-up Language (HTML), that enabled different documents to be linked to others in a process that became known as 'hyperlinking'. As Berners-Lee pointed out in his own reflections on the origins of the web, 'The real world of high-energy physics was one of incompatible networks'. HTML specified how content could be delivered ('packet switched' between client and server) and reassembled in readable form on a web browser. The emergence of the web illustrates another aspect of the Internet's capacity to be neutral and open. Any document could be linked to any other. Any document published on the web was potentially available to anyone with a browser.

Remarkably, Berners-Lee initially found it difficult to convince anyone that the idea was useful – computer experts just did not get it. Crucially, he persuaded his employer CERN to release the web and its browser to the public for free. This act of benevolence proved important. Parallel developments at the University of Minnesota had led to another Internet protocol called Gopher that acted like a listing service, enabling users to view files held on other network servers. However, as the use of Gopher spread around the world, the university treated the system as a commercial spin-out from research activity with an eye to charging a fee to use the platform. Unlike the WWW, which was non-proprietary and did not require a licence, Gopher soon priced itself out of the running to become the standard protocol for surfing the Net. The web was simpler to use, more dynamic in the way it linked documents, and crucially was free to use and develop. It is for this reason that many Internet users continue to 'hold the faith' that the web should be free and open, built as it is on a neutral network. In many aspects and areas of the web, this philosophy still holds true. The rise of weblogs (blogging), for example, is indicative of the free and open access instilled in the early ethics of the web and its use. It is also the belief that the circulation of information and ideas is important for creativity and that the web offers many ways of doing this collaboratively, drawing on the work of others. The political philosophy of such meritocratic access has also been the main motivator behind criticism levelled at any development that threatens this freedom. The enclosure of certain areas of the web by intellectual-property rights is one such area where web activists have been strong. In the next two sections of this chapter, we shall look at how this process is happening across the two most pertinent areas of intellectual property regarding the Internet – copyright and trademark.

The Internet and copyright

At the forefront of challenges to traditional copyright holders – the corporate world of music, film, publishing and television, as well as new cultural industries such as the games industry – has been the rise of the Internet. As a network of networks that brings together computer users from around the world, it carries with it immense powers to liberate people's ability to create and share. The Internet as a global information system can transform our perception of what is possible in a digital environment.

Digitalisation produces some fundamental problems for copyright protection and regulation. Branscomb identifies the fact that existing laws which attempt to protect intellectual property are increasingly stretched in the 'information age':

> As a consequence, many of us are becoming apprehensive that we may not derive income from the intellectual labours that produce the valuable information assets of the information age. We are also concerned about the unauthorised commercial use of facts over which we seemingly have no control and for which there seems to be no viable legal protection. (Branscomb, 1994: 7)

Confusion regarding copyright in the digital environment is most prevalent with the transnational transfer of creative content and information on the Internet. Here, material is being moved for both commercial and private reasons, much of which includes authored works. Digital media, including musical works, multimedia, audio-visual files, media-playing software and database information can all be transferred on the Internet. Underlying the flow of digital media on the Internet is the inherent process of copying, as data is passed from one computer to the next. If we reintroduce the scenario of reproducing a photograph in digital form that we discussed in Chapter 3, we can see that the transfer of digital media entails a series of 'copies' having to be made:

1. The modems at the receiving and transmitting computers will 'buffer' each byte of data that combines to complete the photograph;
2. The 'router' (the network system) will transfer the photograph from one location to another;

3. The receiving computer will automatically copy the photograph within its Random Access Memory (RAM);
4. The photograph may well appear through a web browser (i.e. Netscape Navigator, Microsoft Explorer or Safari);
5. A video decompression chip will unpack the digital version of the photograph to boost the quality of what is viewed;
6. The computer screen will display the photograph;
7. The photograph might eventually be stored on the computer's hard disk; and
8. The photograph might ultimately be printed to produce a 'hard copy'.

The potential to create copies during the simple process of transferring digital media poses the question of whether or not, in the various stages of transmission, copyright may have been infringed. As we have already noted, traditional copyright is based on the protection of 'tangible copies'. This would make step 8 the most visible form of copyright infringement. But, in the processes 1 to 7 above, it is difficult to ascertain whether a tangible copy has been made and, if so, where it resides at any given time.

Part of the problem is caused by the means by which the Internet moves information around. Unlike analogue systems, where information is transferred in a continuous wave, digital media break down the message into fragmented units or packets that are transported as discrete units. This is known as 'packet switching'. The question becomes: does the movement of each 'packet' through the network constitute a reproduction of the work? Should the law consider the partial interim storage of an image as a reproduction of the whole work? So far, these questions have not been adequately resolved, at least not unambiguously. We must now turn to recent international treaties and to national and community legislation to discover how these problems are being resolved.

Legislating for 'temporary copies' and 'safe harbours'

The WIPO Copyright Treaty viewed the 'indirect' and 'temporary' copies of a work held within computer networks as copyrighted material. As the Agreed Statement in Article 7 of the Treaty makes clear:

> The reproduction right, as set out in Article 9 of the Berne Convention, and the exceptions permitted thereunder, fully apply in the digital environment, in particular to the use of works in digital form. It is understood that the storage of a protected work in digital form in an electronic medium constitutes a reproduction within the meaning of Article 9 of the Berne Convention.

The statement clearly intends to include digital copies within the reproduction right. At the time of the Agreement, the Treaty presented a dilemma for telecommunication companies and Internet service providers (ISPs), which were faced with a significant level of liability for the interim copying of copyright works within their networks. Conversely, producers of digital media – software manufacturers, publishers, entertainment companies and the music industry – welcomed this interpretation. The Treaty dismissed the 'open-ended' approach to temporary copies and the maverick approach of many Internet users who viewed the Internet as a 'free for all' medium. When websites are discovered to be disregarding copyright, Internet providers are duty-bound to stop hosting the sites at the request of the rights holder.

The WIPO Copyright Treaty, therefore, makes the reproduction right include all digital copies. It does, however, make certain exceptions to infringement. Temporary digital storage is tolerated on the premise that network providers must make copies in the very functioning of the network itself: reproduction is intrinsic to the process of transferring information. Again, liability is withheld purely on an understanding – a 'gentlemen's agreement' – between network providers and copyright holders.

Similar anomalies exist with the WIPO Performances and Phonogrammes Treaty that attempts to ensure the performer's exclusive right of 'authorising' the direct or indirect reproduction of their performance fixed in phonorecordings. 'Fixation' is broadly agreed to mean the 'embodiment of sounds' and would include the storage of sound in a computer's RAM under this definition.

The question of how the above treaties are read is dependent on the level of volition on the part of network providers. If an ISP was seen to be promoting or knowingly transferring copyrighted material, then rights holders would be able to enforce copyright protection. However, proving that network providers are liable for copyright infringement is not clear-cut, and the law has been unable to find suitable mechanisms to resolve the matter unambiguously. Both the USA and the EU have attempted to qualify the issue of liability with differing degrees of success.

The DMCA takes a 'soft touch' approach to the liability of ISPs, creating various 'safe harbours' that immunise network providers from civil or criminal proceedings. This runs in the face of the pressures to shore up all areas of copyright from the huge copyright lobby led by major Hollywood studios, recording companies and computer-games manufacturers. The US copyright legislation, therefore, takes heed of some of the critical voices of existing copyright law as it is applied to new digital-media industries, recognising the need to introduce specific legislation that meets the explicit needs of new-media systems like the Internet. As with the general mien of the WIPO treaties, the Act ensures that ISPs are not liable for copyright infringement if they act in 'good faith' in disconnecting infringing sites or removing violating content under a 'notice and take down' (NTD) timetable. The Act provides four instances where a 'safe harbour' is made available to ISPs. They include where ISPs are:

- acting as a mere conduit for infringing information;
- caching information in intermediate and temporary storage through an automatic technical process;
- innocent agents in the storage of infringing information; and
- unknowingly linking to an infringing location.

The definition of 'safe harbour' does leave some ambiguities. ISPs are still likely to be brought to court by copyright holders where the network provider is viewed to be colluding in the infringement of copyright. Alternatively, they might be simply lying about their knowledge of infringing websites. The ambiguities in the current Act have placed the onus on case law. There have been a series of landmark cases in the USA regarding copyright infringement by network providers, most of them predating the new legislation. Direct, contributory and vicarious forms of liability have been used to establish infringement by ISPs. The definition of direct liability speaks for itself, where a network provider knowingly infringes the rights of the owner. Contributory liability is a little more complex, but implies that the network provider has knowingly supported the infringement of copyright by a third party. Finally, vicarious liability refers to the economic gain through the activity of a third party who is infringing the rights of a copyright owner. Liability in this area, then, is largely based on the knowledge of infringement on the side of the system operator, or signs of direct commercial gain.

In *Religious Technology Center v Netcom On-line Communication Services*, Netcom was the service provider of a bulletin-board service which posted copyright works of the RTC. Netcom neither created nor controlled the content of the information available to bulletin-board subscribers, nor did it take action to remove the copyright work once the RTC informed it that the bulletin board was posting infringing material. The court had to rule whether or not direct liability for incidental copies automatically made on the network's computers by a third party made the ISP liable. Neither Netcom nor the bulletin-board service was found to be liable. The court ruled that Netcom's system – which automatically and uniformly created temporary copies of all data sent to it – operated much like a photocopying machine that lets the public make copies with it. The

ISP was not seen to be liable because it performed no volitional act to facilitate the infringement but simply allowed its system to be used for posting. However, because Netcom had been warned about the infringement and had refused to act, it would have been liable for contributory infringement. The case was settled in 1996 prior to the DMCA, and Netcom has since set a range of terms and conditions that bind its users to abide by its guidelines on copyright.

In the European context, ISPs have not received such specific safe harbours as under the DMCA. The Copyright Directive does handle the controversial issue of transient reproduction held in computer networks, with exceptions provided from liability for copies made as integral parts of the technological process of transferring information and where copying has no independent economic significance. This latter provision is left to sovereign states to judge and may cause some variance in interpretation and application. There has certainly been increased pressure on ISPs to act promptly where copyright holders believe that a website is infringing its rights. Action has been bolstered by the EU's E-Commerce Directive (00/31/EC), which ensures that ISPs have to respond to activities they know to be infringing copyright. In 2002, the Business Software Alliance issued more than 4,000 'notice and take down' requests to ISPs suspected of hosting websites that enabled 'pirated' copies of software to be downloaded (www.bsa.org).

Legislative pressure of this kind has made ISPs increasingly nervous of their role as regulators of online content. It creates an additional burden that potentially threatens their commercial viability, particularly where they are host to widescale copyright infringement by users whose actions could be read as mass disobedience born of wider cultural values of sharing copyright works for a whole host of reasons. From the point of view of web developers and users, the monitoring of content might also be viewed as an infringement of privacy under human-rights legislation and impinging on freedom of expression. Further legislation introduced to combat copyright infringement, the Intellectual Property Rights Enforcement Directive, allows the media industry to civilly prosecute consumers for relatively minor and non-commercial infringements. The Directive was primarily focused on the criminal counterfeit of media products, but its wording widens the scope of copyright holders to pursue individual cases of seemingly innocuous forms of private copying via the Internet. Personal information on copyright infringers can be forcibly disclosed, and ISPs could potentially have their servers and other equipment seized by the authorities as evidence in any criminal prosecution. ISPs remain in the middle of an ongoing struggle in the balance between copyright holders and end users of information.

Hyperlinking and reuse of copyright material

Hyperlinking is the architectural lifeblood of the Internet. Without it, surfing the web would not be possible. However, there are instances where hyperlinking could be deemed an infringement of copyright. In 1995, the *Shetland News* was launched by journalist Jonathan Wills as an online news magazine. After only a couple of months, the web page was receiving over 2,000 hits per day, a relatively high number given the population of the islands and the level of Internet use at this time. The *Shetland Times*, a long-standing regional newspaper, decided to post some of its content online in February 1996. As a portal to all information about the area, the *Shetland News* included several links to the *Shetland Times* site using the headlines that featured in the electronic version of the newspaper. By selecting a headline, the reader could be connected to that headline on the *Shetland Times'* website. In 1996, the *Shetland Times* sought an injunction against Wills and his website, as the headlines were viewed as copyright works in themselves, being strongly connected to the rest of the newspaper article. The newspaper claimed that the action presented a vital test for the law and the meaning of electronic rights. The case centred on the question of whether or not a publisher retains copyright in the material they publish when it is subsequently put online. The paper held that it did and that, by linking directly to the *Shetland Times'* online articles, Wills may have given the impression to the public that he had generated the news or had some ownership over it. The case was finally settled out of court, but it raised serious questions as to whether permission needs to be granted before a website links to another. Wills had countered that, in the spirit of freedom of information and access, he had made links to the *Shetland Times* in good faith. Wills also pointed out that links to CNN, *The Herald* in Glasgow and numerous other online news sites had not engendered such controversy and legal action. It would have been interesting to see the outcome of the case, as hyperlinks of this kind are universally used on the web. The copying of headlines may have been inappropriate, but the principle of directing web users to other sites is probably one of the most important functions of web browsing.

The issue of ownership of electronic rights was raised in another landmark case involving the *New York Times* and one of its journalists, Jonathan Tasini. Tasini was the president of the US National Writers' Union and argued that the *New York Times* did not have the right to convert stories from the print version into digital databases such as the news aggregator Lexis/Nexis without his prior permission. Further, he argued that release agreements signed by freelance journalists did not cover the new database technology and, therefore, the *New York Times* had engaged in copyright infringement. The *New York Times* argued that it had the rights to the 'collective work' and that placing the content in digital format was a revision, which is privileged under Section 201(c) of the Copyright Act. The strength of Tasini's claim was the licence revenues received by the newspaper, none of which found their way back to the journalist as royalty payments. The Supreme Court ruled that the digital databases did constitute a substantial material change in the work. If the journalist held the copyright to their work, then the newspaper was liable to obtain a licence to sell that work on again to another service. After the ruling, publishers quickly purged many freelance articles from their databases in case of liability. The case was brought in 1993 but not decided until 2001, and publishers subsequently made contractual moves for authors to release rights in newspapers databases. The case brought a realisation that publishers must contractually include electronic rights and foresee future uses of such works when commissioning articles. The *New York Times* had started to do this post-1995, but Tasini had claimed infringement before these clauses came in.

The case also raised some interesting issues around the worth of old information that appears in online databases. As a cultural commons, it could be argued that knowledge of this kind is very important as a historic record of events, but their commercial value may not be as easily identified. In the Tasini case, neither publishers or the freelance journalist could come to an amicable economic solution as to the worth of articles that reside in such databases. While the court ruling attempted to redress the balance of rights between authors and media companies as well as public access to digital information, in practice the power of the media industry won out. Journalists now sign away such rights as a matter of course, enabling media companies to leverage their value through secondary-rights sales.

Of course, the Internet also enables the reuse and retransmission of other forms of media. Webcasting is becoming an increasingly common aspect of the web, with the development of both improved media-playing technologies and more widespread broadband access. Productions produced for webcasts clearly retain the same rights as other forms of content on the Internet, but they differ in one crucial respect from traditional broadcasts. Television broadcasts are bound by territorial-rights agreements. Because the television marketplace is characterised by economic windowing of territories, producers seek to leverage economic value from every licence to broadcast. Broadcast signals must respect national boundaries as much as possible. Where they do not, such as in a satellite 'footprint' extending beyond territorial boundaries, it can lead to legal challenges regarding an infringement of broadcast rights. Webcasting is no respecter of territorial borders. The Internet is global by default, and anything placed on the web is, nominally, available for all the web surfers of the world to see. When a television broadcast is retransmitted via the Internet, it potentially infringes both the right to broadcast in a particular territory and the retransmission right of the host nation's producer. Retransmission of broadcasts via the web is therefore heavily policed. As already highlighted, the economics of both the film and international television-rights markets is premised on windowing and the ability to leverage value from as many different markets as possible. If movies and programmes were made available via the web, then these distinct markets and the ability to price-discriminate between them evaporates in one swoop.

There is an issue of quality here, in that even broadband connections, at least up to 1GB, are no match in quality compared to even analogue television broadcasts. But the technology and potential are there to view television from around the world. Because of the immense value received from film and television licensing, this technological possibility has been strongly resisted. For example, a Canadian webcaster, iCraveTV, retransmitted free-to-air Canadian television via the web, permitted under Canadian copyright legislation (Litman, 2001). However, the US networks and Hollywood in particular baulked at the idea of Canadian television attracting American viewers, including the public performance of Hollywood movies without a US licence. iCraveTV was forced to pull the webcasts, but it showed the potential of the web to deliver new and varied content to a potentially global audience. In contrast, radio broadcasts which carry near-zero economic value in terms of international licensing have blossomed on the web, with thousands of radio stations now available via the web.

WIPO has responded to the threat of the reproduction of broadcasts by introducing a new proposal to extend reproduction rights of broadcasters in the digital age. Released in April 2004, the proposal updates protection afforded to broadcast signals, especially the ability to reproduce and rebroadcast material on the web. Further protection is also to be given to any digital rights-management measures that broadcasters might use to protect their new-media rights. Crucially, WIPO's argument is that older works that are digitally remastered for DVD or Internet streaming are given an additional fifty years' protection to prohibit copying and retransmission. Therefore, any broadcast material entering the public domain could soon find its way back into copyright protection once it has been digitally enhanced in some way (for example, placed in an online digital archive). This regressive step, which potentially outlaws the common practice of copying material from a TV set to tape or record-able DVD, is very problematic. As new-media journalist John Naughton asserted when reviewing the proposal:

> When I first saw the draft (it was published in April), I assumed it must have been written by executives at Fox, NBC and other US TV networks while high on cocaine, because it read like a wish-list of everything a failing industry could want to protect it from the future. (Naughton, 2004)

We have only scratched the surface of the many complications which the Internet raises for copyright holders. In Chapter 3, we noted that digital media and the instantaneous nature of digital distribution mean that reproducing information and disseminating it is easier and faster than ever before. Similarly, in Chapter 4, we observed the realisation of this process in the rise of peer-to-peer file-sharing networks such as Napster that have challenged the ability of media corporations to control their commercial rights. In this chapter, we have seen that there are subtle problems to be resolved regarding the very nature of copying within computer networks and what constitutes an infringement. We have also noted that the balance between creator (author) and producer (media company) of media content has been altered by the rise of the web and has introduced new rights that can prove contentious in terms of ownership.

The Internet and trademarks

As Howkins (2001: 68) notes, the 'growth of brands and other trade marks is the most noticeable symptom of global consumerism'. As the Internet and the evolution of e-commerce have shown, brands remain vitally important for competitive advantage in an increasingly global market-place. Brands rely on their symbolic power to draw attention to them-selves and build an 'acknowledged capacity for value creation' (Castells, 2001: 76). For media companies, the power of the brand is vitally important to promote their service, and for consumers it is an impor-tant symbol of origin and cultural identity. Brands can secure their sym-bolic importance legally through trademark registration and, crucially in the age of the Internet, through the registration of that trademark as a domain name. A domain name is the mnemonic alphanumerical value of digital code, and acts as an address. Host computers are given a unique identifier comprising four groups of numbers (the IP address), and this address is converted to the familiar URL (uniform resource locator) that we are all familiar with when surfing the web. The domain-name system (DNS) operates on a hierarchical format, with top-level domains being most valued (such as .com and .org). The whole system is regulated by the Internet Corporation for Assigned Names and Numbers (ICANN). ICANN is a non-profit private organisation with responsibility for the regulation of a public resource (the DNS) and has therefore come under criticism for abuse of its powerful position at the centre of one of the most crucial aspects of the Internet's architecture (Boyle, 2000a). Domain names continue to be sold by registered agents of ICANN. In the UK, it is currently Nominet, which does not help the suspicion that private, commercial interests dominate the distribution of names on the Internet.

A top-level domain is crucial to global corporations, as it signifies their position in the Internet hierarchy and acts like a respectable address or postcode that everyone expects and is familiar with. Many people using the Internet may try to guess a major company's URL, and ownership of such obvious domain names becomes increasingly imperative and a valuable corporate asset. Moreover, in the context of the media industry, domain names are not only used as a location for a website but also form an important part of marketing communications more generally. Television and radio organisations use their sites to enhance audience interaction and also to promote further news and information about their programmes more generally. For this reason, large media organisations go to extreme lengths to ensure that they own the rights to domains that fit closely with their existing trademarks or other business identifiers. For example, one of the most visited websites in the UK is run by the BBC. Their main URL is bbc.co.uk, which the Corporation registered very early on in the evolution of the web. However, other URLs which might also be associated with the BBC were not initially registered and were captured, sometimes legitimately, by other organisations. The BBC has fought legal and commercial battles with the registered owners of the domain names bbc.com, bbcnews.com, bbc1.com, bbc2.com and bbc.org. In the dispute over bbc.com, the domain was formerly registered by Boston Business Computing of the USA. After unsuccessful legal pressure, the BBC paid a reputed £200,000 for ownership of the domain. The rights purchase raised issues regarding the appropriate use of licence-payers' funds, especially given that bbc.com would automatically transfer to the BBC's main home page bbc.co.uk. Other disputes were arguably more appropriate, whereby the registration of bbc1.com and bbc2.com were deliberate attempts to extort money from the Corporation. Commonly known as cybersquatting, the registration in 'bad faith' is viewed as a predatory practice and is used either to direct customers away from a well-known trademark holder's site, or as a means of extorting money for the domain name to be to assigned back to the major brand.

Disputes over domain names have become increasingly prevalent as trademark owners attempt to wrest control of the various domain names that appear to make reference to their organisation. In 1999, ICANN established a domain-name resolution service operated under the auspices of WIPO. The resolution service is designed to avoid litigation and private injunctions and to come to an independent judgement over claims to a name. One of the most disputed areas is the registration of domain names relating to famous celebrities. As we discussed in Chapter 7, celebrity image rights are viewed as valuable assets in the media and promotional industries, and control of personal websites is seen as an essential part of that process. Stars such as Robbie Williams and Billy Connolly in the UK, and Julia Roberts and the estate of Jimi Hendrix in the USA, have been successful in countering cybersquatters through the ICANN resolution procedures. Ownership of personal domain names has also become important within contractual negotiations between stars and their employers. Footballers such as David Beckham have assigned their rights to football clubs to control, and in the music industry Sony made moves to include company ownership of artists' domain names and any variants for life within their standard contracts. Such extreme clauses present problems when stars change employers – in this case football clubs or record labels – setting up a potentially bizarre situation where ownership of the domain remains with a previous employer.

The relation between trademarks and domain names is problematic because, as with other aspects of the Internet and the law, trademarks are not international but are territorially bound. In the EU, this may be countered by applying for a European trademark, which provides reciprocity across nations in the EU but does not prevent similar domains from being snapped up in other parts of the world. Similarly, a dispute involving the artist Madonna went to arbitration when a Tunisian company registered 'Madonna' as a trademark in that country and bought the domain name madonna.com. The Tunisian website made clear through a disclaimer that the site was not associated with the pop singer. Nevertheless, the arbitration panel decided to transfer the domain name to the singer because of the likelihood of confusion and the fact that the Tunisian company had registered the name in bad faith. The decision raised alarm that any claim to a domain name by a famous celebrity or major media company would automatically receive the benefit of the panel's decision. The case and others like it reveal the power of global brands to roll over the interests of what might otherwise be seen as legitimate registrations. At the international level, where two or more trademarks of the same name exist, it would appear that the economically powerful US or European-owned media tend to receive the benefit of the resolution process. This imbalance of power is made all the more evident given cross-industry collaborations such as the Copyright Coalition on Domain Names (CCDN), which operates to lobby on behalf of the copyright industries, and bodies such as the Business Software Alliance (BSA), the Motion Picture Association of America (MPAA), the Recording Industry Association of America (RIAA), the Software and Information Industry Association (SIIA), the two largest organisations administering the performance right in musical compositions (ASCAP and BMI), and major copyright-owning companies such as Time Warner and the Walt Disney Company.

The moves to tighten and harmonise the fit between trademarks and domain names are problematic. Although, as suggested above, many of us make intuitive guesses to find web addresses, more often than not we bring up a search engine such as Google and click on the link we have found. This does not require that we need to know the URL, and if we bookmark the site it can easily be found again. The use of web addresses in promotions and television programming does point towards the importance of a close association between domain names and brands, but under trademark law this is not a good enough reason to enjoy ubiquitous protection. As Azmi (2000: 213) has argued, trademarks are important agents 'for the creation of goodwill, imprinting upon the public mind an anonymous and impersonal guarantee of satisfaction'. Where media companies and celebrities are overly pernicious in their attempts to wrest domain names from others, sometimes from fans with a genuine interest in a film, programme or star, more harm is potentially done to this goodwill than would otherwise be the case. The message it sends out is negative, proprietorial and against wider use of the Internet commons.

Conclusion

The Internet is a phenomenal resource. In terms of the circulation of information and the potential for mass creativity and innovation, we have not seen anything like it before in our history. Yet, intellectual property coupled with technological protection measures discussed in Chapter 3 are binding this surge in creativity through restrictive regulation practices and laws. There is one aspect of intellectual-property law pertinent to the regulation of the Internet that we have not touched upon in this chapter, and that is patents. We have analysed the way in which a neutral network has become an integral facet of the web's architecture and democratic potential. In June 2001, this neutral network was potentially threatened by a lawsuit brought by British Telecom against Prodigy, one of the first of the web's ISPs and owned by the second largest telecoms company in the USA, SBC. BT claimed to have found a 'lost' patent in its archives that revealed rights to one of the central planks of the web itself, hyperlinking. Originally filed in 1976, the patent was granted in 1989. BT planned to seek licensing fees from US Internet providers for the use of its invention, backdating the licence to 1989. BT's patent describes its 1970s Prestel 'View Data' teletext and videotext service, which used links to route users of a dynamic viewdata technology from one viewpoint page to another (a 'hidden page'). The US Internet community was incredulous at the lawsuit and criticised BT's claim as groundless and subject to 'prior art' (where previous hyperlinks technology existed). BT ultimately lost the suit in August 2002 when the court ruled that the patent for the 'hidden page' bore no resemblance to the contemporary practice of hyperlinking. Although software patents have been vehemently resisted in the UK (although a European directive being put through by the European Council in 2004 may change this), they are available under US legislation. Many of the leading Internet companies have sought to gain from licensing specific aspects of code to reap financial reward for developing new Internet-related software. Patents exist for search engines (AltaVista), one-click technology for online sales (Amazon.com), online reverse auctions (Priceline.com) and measuring Internet advertising (DoubleClick).

All this moves away from the original open source and free software ideals of the early pioneers of the Internet. In the US context, lawsuits abound regarding patent infringement, with many smaller software developers taking on giants like Microsoft for including specific applications in their browsers, media players or operating systems in the hope of winning significant financial damages. For this reason, Microsoft and others covet the source code of their applications ever more tightly in an attempt to restrict access to how their systems work. Technological restrictions are bolstered by intellectual-property rights and prevent the potential of genuine innovators to produce interoperable software that works across different platforms and provides competition to Microsoft's dominant position in the software industry. As we shall discuss in the final chapter, how media organisations negotiate the challenges of the Internet and the technological and legal constraints increasingly imposed on the use of content becomes an important question for media analysts more generally. New technologies bring with them new issues, but interestingly old choices are having to be made between private ownership of media rights and the wider interest of the public and the cultural commons.

Study question

Given that digital technologies allow perfect copies to be made, and the ability to produce and distribute content is increasingly easy, is there a case for dispensing with the notion of copyright altogether to allow for the free flow of information?

Further reading

Goldstein, P. (2003), *Copyright's Highway: From Gutenberg to the Celestial Jukebox*, Stanford: Stanford University Press.
Lessig, L. (2001), *The Future of Ideas: The Fate of the Commons in a Connected World*, New York: Random House.

Relevant links

Pamela Samualson homepage – http://www.sims.berkeley.edu/%7Epam/papers.html
Jessica Liman homepage – http://www.law.wayne.edu/litman/
James Boyle homepage – http://james-boyle.com/
Lawrence Lessig homepage – http://cyberlaw.stanford.edu/lessig/
Wired Magazine – http://www.wired.com
O'Reilly Network – http://www.oreillynet.com/

9 Conclusion: media rights and the commons

The street finds its own use for the law of unintended consequences. Technology will change the way the copyright industry makes its ungodly sums of money, but it won't eliminate it. No one can predict what the innovative ways of selling entertainment will be – that's innovation for you – but it will come.

(Cory Doctorov, 2002)

I don't agree with the copyright laws and I don't have a problem with people downloading the movie and sharing it with people as long as they're not trying to make a profit off my labour. I would oppose that. I do well enough already and I made this film because I want the world to change. The more people who see it the better, so I'm happy this is happening. Is it wrong for someone who's bought a film on DVD to let a friend watch it for free? Of course it's not. It never has been and never will be. I think information, art and ideas should be shared.

(Documentary activist Michael Moore, quoted in Bruce, 2004)

Introduction

One of the major cinematic releases for summer 2004 in the UK was *A Cinderella Story*, directed by Mark Rosman and released by Warner Brothers. The film epitomises the ways in which popular culture draws on existing ideas, in this case extracting the storyline from possibly the most famous fairytale in history, and making something new. *Cinderella*, or *A Little Glass Slipper*, a story from European folklore originally captured in print by the French poet Charles Perrault in 1697, has been retold many times in film and television, including George Melies' *Cendrillon*, released in 1899, and the Walt Disney animation *Cinderella*, released in 1949. The story has endured on film not only because it is a fantastic story of love over adversity, but also because it is in the public domain – free and open for anyone to use, adapt and make their own. As it happens, the modernist twists of *A Cinderella Story*, substituting mobile phone for glass slipper as the heroine's true mark of identity, failed to capture the imagination of critics and audiences alike (although it still managed to gross more than $13.5m during its opening weekend). Nevertheless, the point to be made is that all creativity in contemporary media draws on the well of ideas already circulating in a culture, the skill is in doing it innovatively. In the case of *Cinderella*, there is no need to pay for derivative licences and adaptation rights. It is, literally, a 'gift to the public'.

However, arguments about the value of the public domain to Hollywood and its industry representatives at the MPAA would probably fall on deaf ears. In Hollywood's terms, what is sauce for the goose is not so good for the gander. Disney's 1949 version of *Cinderella* only grossed $30m in its lifetime at the box office, but it has since generated several times that amount in secondary rights for video and DVD and in licences for merchandising and other commercial spin-offs. Under current US law, the film will be protected by copyright until 2044. Lessig (2004: 22) has noted how Disney's 'spark of creativity' has been 'built upon the work of others'. But, because of the way in which modern copyright operates, using the animated version of *Cinderella* – or any of Disney's 'creations' – is blocked. In spite of the fact that the film was created more than half a century ago, it is not available (except maybe for exorbitant and massively prohibitive licence fees) to provide that same 'spark' to become the innovative building blocks of contemporary creatives. So if, for example, you wanted to produce an experimental short digital film made available for downloading via the Internet using excerpts from all the existing Cinderella films currently available, patchworked together to create an innovative telling of the ancient fairytale, you would be stopped in your tracks by copyright. Even if you made a claim that the 'sampling' of films in this way created a new aesthetic – a Cinderella remix, if you like – your way would remain barred.

It is difficult to gauge whether sampling a film in this way would damage the commercial value of the original film. There are strong arguments to suggest that a director's moral rights and their integrity might be compromised; but such rights have never been taken seriously by Hollywood because the producer's commercial rights have always taken precedent. However, as Drahos and Braithwaite argue, the opportunities afforded by new-media technologies present some new areas of emphasis for the use of copyright works: 'More broadly, one could argue that in a world where works can be digitized, seamlessly integrated with others and communicated instantaneously to millions, the principles of paternity and integrity become more important to authors rather than less' (Drahos and Braithwaite, 2003: 176).

Although altering an original film may infringe the moral rights of the creator – as has happened with the colorisation of some black-and-white films from the 1940s and 1950s – surely in some cases the reuse of content in new ways might actually invigorate interest in the original films, making them more commercially desirable? This has certainly happened in the music industry, where sampled tracks have gained a new lease of life after being discovered by a new, younger audience (Goodwin, 1990). One consequence of copyright lockout is the deterrence of creativity. In the context of music, where this battle has raged hardest, Greenfield and Osborne (2004: 95) note: 'Given the existence of intellectual property rights, future uses of music works can be fettered on the grounds that someone owns the originals and can therefore control their reuse'. As we shall discover later in this chapter, this is an important observation because, in the age of the Internet and the wizardry of digital media, the potential for innovation and media creativity is arguably more expansive than any period in our cultural history. Before moving on to discuss the new possibilities afforded by digital media and the development of open and progressive media-rights initiatives, we first need to assess why the media industry's obsession with copyright infringement and piracy is potentially damaging to our media culture.

Piracy paranoia

Numerous authors (Boyle, 1997; Litman, 2001; Lessig, 2001 and 2004; Vaidhyanathan, 2001; Drahos and Braithwaite, 2002) have highlighted the manner in which intellectual-property laws are increasingly twisted, stretched and ultimately compromised to fit the needs of giant media corporations. Through hard-nosed lobbying and persuasion, these corporations put enough pressure on legislatures for intellectual-property rights to become extended in order to shore up the valued assets of the media industry. Moreover, where copyright is threatened by the powerful tools available in the digital age to manipulate, reproduce and distribute media content, new legislation is at hand to support digital locks and prevent their circumvention.

The media industries claim that new legislative measures are needed to curb the levels of piracy that they see as harming their businesses. The recording industry makes claims that one-third of the CDs sold around the world are counterfeit. The music industry makes even further claims for what it terms 'business leakage' from MP3 downloads, with estimates of the value of losses wavering between $300m and $700m. The widening of broadband Internet access around the world has also led the film-industry lobby, the MPAA, to make similar claims for infringement of film copyright. In July 2004, a monitoring study published by the MPAA claimed that one-quarter of the world's broadband users had illegally downloaded a film and that film piracy in general was costing them £3.5bn in lost revenue on an annual basis (*The Guardian*, 9 July 2004).

The film industry has been one of the most vehement defenders of copyright. The pattern of this concern for copyright infringement, especially of derivative works, has a long history. As Vaidhyanathan (2001) recalls, the US Copyright Act of 1909 introduced the concept of corporate copyright initially with the premise of protecting the interests of the publishing industry. However, these new rights soon conferred a new power to the emerging film studios beginning to form in Hollywood. Vaidhyanathan (2001: 102) notes:

> In the case of film production companies, corporate copyright allowed studio control of content, distribution, advertising and derivative products. Directors, producers, screenwriters, and even actors – all of whom could philosophically claim 'authorship' of a film – regularly sign away control of their work to a studio, and cannot claim the benefits and privileges of legal authorship.

It is therefore the corporate film industry that pursues copyright infringement and not the creative 'authors' of the film. In the UK, the Federation Against Copyright Theft (FACT), part of the wider Alliance Against Counterfeiting and Piracy (AACP), has investigated and pursued counterfeit film media in collaboration with the police, customs and excise and trading-standards authorities. Watch most videos or DVDs rented in the UK and you will see a copyright notice and a public-information advertisement by FACT warning against film piracy and its reported connections with organised crime and terrorism. Similarly, public statements by industry executives frequently refer to the damage being done to Hollywood's production community, drawing on the utilitarian philosophy of copyright to argue that piracy undermines the incentive to create. Take, for example, the following quote from James Spertus, the head of anti-piracy at the MPAA, who cried: 'Hundreds of people have put tens of thousands of hours into making a truly great picture, and the notion of having it stolen and sent out for free around the world is just plain wrong' (quoted in *The Guardian*, 1 July 2004).

The rhetoric of this statement draws on the mistaken belief that production staff and many of the artists benefit from the box-office receipts and secondary-rights royalties. The statement masks the facts that the fight against copyright infringement more strongly represents corporate interests of the film industry and that the moral claim to the damage done to the artisans of the film-making process is completely disingenuous. These alarmist campaigns also represent a strategy to win the hearts and minds of the public against so-called 'piracy' through an association with serious criminal behaviour. As with the music, games and software industries, the film industry annually reveals figures announcing the potential lost revenues through 'piracy'. The reputed figures for the UK ranged from £400m (AACP) to £500m (British Video Association) lost in revenue from piracy and counterfeiting in 2003. A large portion of this loss is accredited to cinema bootlegging, the videoing of cinematic performances. For consumers, the attraction of bootleg videos and DVDs is the cheapness of the copies and the fact that they usually pre-empt official release dates for video and DVD formats. The industry uses a standard six-month differential between the cinematic release of a film and its rental/sale release in a recorded-media format. The economics of release-windowing are being undermined by bootlegging and counterfeiting, and have increased pressure on the distributors to collapse the timing of the two releases in some territories. For example, counterfeit copies of major releases frequently appear in Thailand, Malaysia and China during the same week or even well before cinematic release via the major distributors.

The industry has used several countervailing practices to try to stem the level of infringement. When the third film of the Harry Potter series, *Harry Potter and the Prisoner of Azkaban*, was released by Warner Brothers in June 2004, projectionists and ushers at Vue Cinemas owned by the studio were provided with night-vision goggles to help spot those smuggling camcorders into the theatre (*The Age*, 2004). In Yugoslavia, where the film had not gone on general release, tickets to private screenings of pirated copies of the film were selling for a reputed £30, prompting one distributor to offer a £3,000 reward to any person willing to testify in court against counterfeiters or outlets selling infringing copies (*Ananova*, 2004). Again, the desire to squeeze every commercial ounce out of the film is evident in such desperate measures and masks the huge profits which the studio actually received from the film (in June 2004, *Harry Potter and the Prisoner of Azkaban* earned the third largest opening weekend box-office revenues in the USA, ever, worth a whopping $93m in just three days).

The piracy paranoia that has struck the film industry has even had an effect on its own internal networks of distribution, including pre-release copies sent to members of the Academy of Motion Picture Arts when judging its annual awards ceremony, the Oscars. 'Preview screeners' were viewed as one area of leakiness for pirated copies of major Hollywood films. In 2003, The Academy initially decided to ban screeners amid fears that they were a major source of counterfeit videos and DVDs. They later introduced a watermarking system that identified the recipient of each tape or DVD, enabling the tracking of pirated material back to its source. In 2004, the studios introduced a new solution to protect against copying – specially encrypted DVDs that would only play on compatible players (*The Guardian*, 2004).

There is an irony that through its counteractive practices and copy-protection zeal – what I have called piracy paranoia – the movie industry, and all other copyright industries for that matter, are driving themselves further and further away from their customers. The emphasis on massive financial rewards from a select number of smash hits has produced a series of contradictory processes. The majority of resources are pumped into the minority of commercially elite projects that, once released, demand excessive technological and legal protection to maintain the flow of cash into the copyright holders' coffers. In turn, other projects get sidelined or underpromoted, invariably returning a massive loss to the producers; or, alternatively, potentially great creative ideas hit the cutting-room floor for lack of commercial potential. The top-heavy economics of the copyright industry are arguably depleting our culture rather than enhancing it. In the second half of this chapter, we shall look at new visions of how media rights might best be used to open up creativity and capture the power of new-media technologies, to democratise and enhance the freedom of information, and to make intellectual property work for the common good, not selective private gain.

The commons under fire

The obsessive response to copyright infringement by the media industry brings us back to some broader questions about how information and knowledge circulate in society. In Chapter 2, we acknowledged the philosophical underpinnings of intellectual property as a concept. The battle against piracy draws on the utilitarian philosophy that copyright acts as an incentive to create. It suggests that, without strong and well-enforced property rights, creators lose the will to create. This is the political stick that the media industry uses to usher in new legislation to protect more informational goods for longer periods of time. As we have also seen, it is the moral device which the industry uses to persuade end users of content that their rights are limited and that infringement of copyright causes harm to the wider creative community. But is this really the case? Are there other incentives to creative practice? Would loosening and opening up copyright really lessen the incentive to innovate and introduce new cultural ideas?

Answers to these questions are emerging in the new-media environment, many of the clues coming from sectors of the IT industry. Free software and the open source movement have received wide acclaim as pioneering ways to develop informational goods through the collective management of resources. In Chapter 8, we noted the importance of open collaboration in the development of the Internet as one of the most pow-erful communication tools of our time. This philosophy of free, shared, public access to information continued to influence software develop-ment into the 1980s, but was increasingly being impinged upon by grow-ing commercial pressure from new software giants like IBM, who wanted to protect their interests behind copyright, trade secrets and boilerplate contracts. Recognising the threat to open, creative, software develop-ment, MIT programmer Richard Stallman railed against the increasingly secretive world of source code (the human language of computer soft-ware) and set up the Free Software Foundation in 1985. Stallman worked with Unix, the operating system devised by AT&T in the 1970s and early 1980s to help run its new computer systems, which was open for all to use and develop. However, in 1984, AT&T decided to commercialise Unix, and the source code became locked behind trade secrets and copyright controls. Stallman's response was to release a free version of the software called GNU, a recursive acronym meaning 'GNU's not Unix' (Lessig, 1999).

The important thing about GNU was that it was released as free soft-ware under what Stallman termed a 'copyleft' licence, because it was the antithesis of copyright. The copyleft licences required developers of free software to make publicly available any changes or improvements of the source code for other to use. Cleverly, if anyone tried to privatise the free software, they would automatically violate the copyleft licence (Vaidhyanathan, 2001: 156). The system ensured that developments of free software remained in the public domain in perpetuity. Subsequent developments of GNU led to the Linux operating system, innovated by Finnish student Linus Torvald during the early 1990s. Linux also used the copyleft principle to develop and share ideas, eventually forming what became known as the open source movement. Open source software thrives on the notion of the 'gift economy', whereby you develop new relationships through the mutual sharing of information that is given and received as a gift. There is no ownership of open source software; it is out-side the capitalist market for information and copyright goods. As May (2002: 98) argues, 'the open source software movement may currently represent the most developed political alternative to "normal" society, promoting a real e-mutualism'. While the political motivations of open source users may be quite varied and the power of the movement dis-persed, it nevertheless does represent a challenge to dominant centres of wealth and power in the computing industry.

Another feature of open source software is that mutual checks and peer-regulation mean that fewer mistakes are made as the software develops (unlike commercial software that constantly requires upgrades and patches to make it work). But, most importantly, open source movements have something to contribute to wider cultural production. Open source has social benefits born of the democratic principles it runs on, providing access to information and thereby increasing the likelihood of people to use new technologies. As Boyle (2003) has argued, advocates of intellectual-property rights point towards the economic reasoning behind the 'tragedy of the commons' – the belief that free access to any common resource ultimately leads to overuse and eventual decay because nobody is accountable for its use. Therefore, the argument goes, property rights provide control; they maximise value and benefit those who become the guardians of the rights of access. But open source movements prove that collective control of resources can work effectively and more beneficially than privatised markets for information. This economic rhetoric has dominated the debate over intellectual-property rights and dictated the legal and technological environment within which the media operate.

As we noted in Chapter 3 and again in Chapter 8, the prevalence of extended copyright legislation and the arrival of restrictive DRM – the digital locks – have prompted a backlash to the dominant ideology of intellectual-property rights. At the centre of the critique is the defence and promotion of the public domain and the 'commons' – the well of information free and open to the public to use as they see fit, with new information continually adding to this stock. As Boyle (2003) further points out, economists shirk at the idea of the commons acting as an incentive for creativity and innovation. Economists would argue that information is non-rivalrous and a public good – one web page can be downloaded by one or a million people, but the resource would not be depleted. Economists would also ask: if ideas are infinitely available, where are the incentives to produce new ones? Because information held in the commons is non-rivalrous, would the information commons not lead to underproduction? Capitalism answers these questions by conferring legal monopolies on informational goods to make them exchangeable. If we relate this process to media, it might mean that archived material only sees the light of day again for a fee. For example, many newspapers now charge for access to their electronic archives. Alternatively, music, film and other cultural goods from the early twentieth century might have moved into the public domain – most notably Mickey Mouse – except that legislators have extended the term of copyright to ensure that such media remain in private ownership and only available at a price. Contemporary technological controls mean that today's media products may never be truly open to the public domain in the future because of prohibitive DRM. This means extending control of how people use media beyond their rights under the first-sale doctrine. It means controlling people's behaviour.

We know why this is the case, because digital technology and distribution threatens to make media goods less rivalrous and less excludable. Lessig (1999, 2001) and others (Bollier, 2002; Boyle, 2003) have shown that the media industry's response to this threat has been to increase control over copying, to pursue those who would dare to violate such controls (whether those who run peer-to-peer networks or those who use them) and to persuade us that it is all in the name of creativity and innovation. The struggle against this 'enclosure movement' (Boyle, 2003) is to ensure that the commons is sustained and built upon by new and innovative means. It means having respect for the balance that copyright initially sought to foster, between incentive and the free flow of knowledge and information in the commons for others to build upon. Again, as Boyle has argued, it means creating an environmental movement against the enclosure of information across numerous fronts. One way in which this is happening has been the introduction of new ways of viewing media rights, which we shall now investigate.

The creative commons: 'take a bit and make it new'

The quote by the documentary film-maker Michael Moore at the beginning of this chapter reveals some of the ambivalence that many creatives feel with regard to the non-commercial use of their work. In March 2004, the singer George Michael announced that he would not record another album for commercial release but would instead distribute his music for free via his dedicated website. Michael's reasoning was that he had earned enough from his recording career and no longer wanted the pressure of producing hits. As he revealed in an interview on BBC Radio 1, 'I've been very well remunerated for my talents over the years so I really don't need the public's money' (Booth, 2004). In making this gesture, Michael, no stranger to copyright disputes with major record labels, had revealed part of the copyright bargain between creators and their audience. It goes without saying that he was in a privileged position from which to promise such a gift to his fans; but the sentiment, like Moore's, was important. This sentiment is in contradistinction to the media industry, whose views we have recounted throughout this book. As we have seen, the industry gets very heavy-handed when consumers of media goods infringe their rights, and even more bullish when artists complain about contractual exploitation. But is there another way of looking at this problem? Is it possible to respect the creators of media content while having the opportunity to use it, share it and perhaps make something new and innovative built upon it?

There are both radical and more nuanced answers to these questions. The most radical assertions about the power of the Internet argue that the new age of free information will totally undermine copyright regimes and bypass the distribution networks of corporate media. Unfortunately, this version of 'copyright anarchy', as Marshall and Frith (2004) stress, forgets the fact that creators quite often need publishers (in the widest sense) for their work to reach the public. Moreover, Marshall and Frith (2004: 211) observe that 'those musicians who have most effectively used web communities and by-passed record companies are those who have already got a fan base, are already known to their potential listeners because of the work, however long ago, of a record company'. This point could clearly be equated with the OD2 music download service developed by Peter Gabriel. Nevertheless, as we have seen, the contractual relations between creators and corporate investors in the media industry are heavily biased in favour of the latter. What needs to be reconfirmed through a form of media rights, therefore, is a stronger bond between creator and user that recognises talent and effort at the aesthetic, informational and economic levels of engagement. Furthermore, in the digital age, another leap of faith is needed to accept that users can become producers of media content, which can add again to the commons of ideas and information.

The open source movement and the concept of free software have shown a way in which 'free culture' or 'free media' can exist. The Creative Commons (CC), launched in 2001, enables copyright holders to grant some of their rights to the public while retaining others. A CC licence enables authors of publications and media works to release open content on the web that may be downloaded, copied and reused in various ways. Where copyright makes a claim to all rights being reserved, a CC licence means that some rights are reserved. An electronic tag or piece of metadata can specify the exact licensing terms of an author's work, which may vary depending on the rights the author wants to reserve. But the key to the concept is that information gets to circulate in the public domain far quicker and with fewer restrictions attached than the terms existing under current copyright. The CC website provides examples of its use in a series of online animations, championing authors such as Cory Doctorov, who released his novel for free downloading in parallel with commercial publication, enabling others to translate his work into other languages and musicians who shared music on the web for others to capture, remix and record. The motto that accompanies the CC licences is 'take a bit and make it new' – that is, not to copy but to remix culture. The CC licence therefore potentially breaks down barriers between the author and the consumer and connects culture to wider notions of citizenship. Media works become public assets but may still recoup private profits through associated commercial rights. In this sense, the CC licence is a midway point between strict copyright control and the unprotected public domain. Examples of the CC in action have primarily been from individuals or small-scale publishers; so, is it possible for large corporate media to initiate similar agreements?

In November 2002, one example of the true power of the Internet to deliver information and media on demand, instantaneously without fear of breaking copyright, was realised with the launch of the British Pathé Film Archive, the world's first digital news archive. The archive, owned by ITN News, has placed more than 3,500 hours of newsreel stretching from 1909 to 1970 on the web and was digitised with the assistance of a £50m grant from the UK National Lottery Fund. The premise of the archive's use is to discriminate access for private, educational or commercial use in the following ways:

1. Licences of low-resolution preview files ('Preview Moving Image Files');
2. Licences of high-resolution master files ('High Resolution Moving Image Files');
3. Education Licence for use of high-resolution master files by schools, and local education authorities.

The ability to search through the archive and download a full preview of the film is an amazingly powerful tool for historians and media researchers. Through its tiered licensing agreements, the archive is opened up into the public domain, with more commercial rights being retained.

A further example of large media organisations opening up their archives includes the Creative Archive initiative of the BBC. First mooted by former Director General Greg Dyke during the Edinburgh Film Festival in August 2003, the BBC Creative Archive draws on the philosophy behind the Creative Commons licences and the power of peer-to-peer technology to open up access to the largest and most historic broadcasting archive in the world. After more than a decade of exploiting its cherished programmes through its commercial arm BBC Worldwide, it appeared that the management at the BBC had experienced some kind of epiphany regarding the future of digital media and digital downloading. With advice from Lawrence Lessig and the US Library of Congress archivist Brewster Kahle, the BBC set about releasing its archive into the public domain. Although BBC Worldwide and the secondary-rights revenues which the Corporation has enjoyed from the sale of programmes such as *Teletubbies* and formats like *The Weakest Link* have been very lucrative, the BBC's position as a licence-funded public-service broadcaster also puts other pressures on it to be publicly accountable. The public-service remit of the BBC is the key to understanding why its decision to open up access to its archive is nowhere near as problematic as it would be for a commercial media organisation. As the journalist Danny O'Brian has commented, 'while other media companies worry about too many net users getting hold of their creations for free, the BBC worries about too few' (O'Brian, 2003). Put simply, the more people use BBC programmes, the more its remit under Royal Charter is given credence. Indeed, the strategic move to open up the archive meets specific provisions of its Royal Charter renewed in 1996 to 2006. Enabling programmes that would otherwise rarely see the light of day to be available for downloading is a potentially inspirational resource for future media producers, educationalists and historians. A licence like those created under the Creative Commons principles would also enable these programmes to be reused, edited and remixed to form innovative uses, with the proviso that any new creations are for non-commercial use. In spite of commercial restrictions, the cultural and artistic permutations are vast given the scale of the archive. As the Archive's joint director Paula Le Dieu revealed in May 2004, 'one of the key values of this material was as fuel for the creative endeavours of the nation' (Digital-Lifestyles, 2004).

The Creative Archive neatly shows the potential of unlocking certain media rights into the public domain. Throughout this book, we have seen the various ways in which copyright and other intellectual-property laws have been exploited across the media industry to create vast global media oligarchies. This has largely been achieved through a combination of copyright and contracts ensuring that creators pass over many of their rights to large corporate investors who attempt to leverage as much money as possible from a minority of hits. We have argued in this chapter that the excesses of the media-rights regime have led to a piracy paranoia, where every infringement of copyright is vehemently policed. The new information networks and the wider cultural effects of digitalisation have exacerbated this regulatory zeal to protect content through new laws and technologies. However, media rights may have a positive outcome if the balance in the deal between creators, users and investors is recalibrated. While many people may well use a digital archive to watch old BBC programmes with no intention of remixing them into something new, the promise of initiatives of this kind might also provide avenues for inspiration and innovation, filling some of the creative capacity currently available in the new-media age.

Study question

Why is the public domain important in the age of digital, networked media? How will media rights shape the future of the creative and information commons?

Suggested further reading

Lessig, L. (2004) *Free Culture: How Big Media Uses Technology and the Law to Lock Down Culture and Control Creativity*, New York: Penguin Books. Available under a Creative Commons licence at http://free-culture.org/get-it.

Related websites

http://creativecommons.org/
http://commoncontent.org/
http://www.friendsofthecommons.org/
http://www.archive.org/
http://www.eff.org/
http://ukcdr.org/

Bibliography

ACCC (2001), 'Parallel imports of CDs: Sony provides undertakings to the court'. http://www.accc.gov.au/content/index.phtml/itemId/87686/fromItemId/378012

The Age (2004), 'Potter piracy', 1 June. http://www.theage.com.au/cgi-bin/common/popupPrintArticle.pl?path=/articles/2004/06/01/1086037756669.html

Ananova (2004), 'Movie distributor offers reward for illegal copies of Harry Potter'. http://www.ananova.com/entertainment/story/sm_479209.html

Arnold, R. (2002), 'Copyright in Sporting Events and Broadcasts or Film of Sporting Events after Norowzian', in E. Barendt et al., *The Yearbook of Copyright and Media Law 2002*, Oxford: Oxford University Press, pp. 51–60.

Azmi, I. M. (2000), 'Domain Names and Cyberspace: The Application of Old Norms to New Problems', *International Journal of Law and Information Technology*, 8:2, 193–213.

Barnett, S. (1990), *Games and Sets: The Changing Face of Sport on Television*, London: BFI.

BBC (2002), ' "Legal row" over Bill Wyman name', 15 November. http://news.bbc.co.uk/2/hi/entertainment/2480259.stm

BBC (2004), 'Blockbusters boost UK DVD sales', 8 January. http://news.bbc.co.uk/1/hi/entertainment/film/3380247.stm

Beverley-Smith, H. (2002), *The Commercial Appropriation of Personality*, Cambridge: Cambridge University Press.

Bollier, D. (2002), 'Why the public domain matters: the endangered wellspring of creativity, commerce and democracy'. http://www.publicknowledge.org/content/policy-papers/pic/event-protecting-information-commons-paper2/view

Booth, J. (2004), 'George Michael exhausts his patience with fame', *New Media Guardian*, 11 March. http://media.guardian.co.uk/newmedia/story/0,7496,1166977,00.html

Borland, J. (2003), 'Music industry: piracy is choking sales', *CNET News.com*, 9 April. http://news.com.com/Music+industry:+Piracy+is+choking+sales/2100-1027_3-996205.html

Bower, T. (2003), *Broken Dreams: Vanity, Greed and the Souring of British Football*, London: Simon and Schuster.

Bowman, L. (2003), 'Arguments made in DVD cracking case', *News.com*.

http://news.com.com/Arguments+made+in+DVD-cracking+case/2100-1025_3-1011326.html

Boyd, S. (2003), 'The legal status of a sportsman's image rights'. http://www.selbornechambers.co.uk/site_articles/ Image%20Rights3.doc

Boyle, J. (1997), *Shamens, Software and Spleens: Law and the Construction of the Information Society*, Harvard: Harvard University Press.

Boyle, J. (2000a), 'A Nondelegation Doctrine for the Digital Age?', *Duke Law Journal*, 50:5, 5–16.

Boyle, J. (2000b), 'Analysis, Price Discrimination and Digital Intellectual Property', *Vanderbilt Law Review*, 53:6: 2,007–39.

Boyle, J. (2003), 'The Second Enclosure Movement and the Construction of the Public Domain', *Law and Contemporary Problems*, Winter/Spring 2003, nos 1–2: 33–74. http://www.law.duke.edu/journals/lcp/indexpd.htm

Boyle, R., W. Dinan and S. Morrow (2002), 'Doing the Business? The Newspaper Reporting of the Business of Football', *Journalism*, 3:2, 149–69.

Boyle, R. and R. Haynes (2004), *Football in the New Media Age*, London: Routledge.

Branscomb, A. (1994), *Who Owns Information? From Privacy to Public Access*, New York: Basic Books.

Brook, D. (2004), 'How to get on telly quicker', *Media Guardian*, 9 August.

Bruce, I. S. (2004), 'Moore: pirate my film, no problem'. http://www.sundayherald.com/43167

BTDA (2003), 'BTDA presents to the DCMS and DTI', *News from the BTDA*, August, Issue 8. Available at http://www.btda.org/

BTDA (2004), 'UK TV exports approach $1 billion for the first time', *BTDA Press Release*, 13 May. http://www.btda.org/

Castells, M. (2000), *The Rise of the Network Society*, 2nd edn, Oxford: Blackwell.

Castells, M. (2001), *The Internet Galaxy: Reflections on the Internet, Business and Society*, Oxford: Oxford University Press.

cnn.com (2001), 'Napster: the house that Fanning built', 12 March. http://www.cnn.com/2001/TECH/internet/03/10/cover.napster/

Coombe, R. J. (1992), 'The Celebrity Image and Cultural Identity: Publicity Rights and the Subaltern Politics of Gender', *Discourse: Berkeley Journal for Theoretical Studies in Media and Culture*, 59 (61): 59–88.

Cornish, W. (1999), *Intellectual Property*, 4th edn, London: Sweet & Maxwell.

Correa, C. M. (2000), *Intellectual Property Rights, the WTO and Developing Countries: The TRIPS Agreement and Policy Options*, London: Zed Books.

DCMS (1999), *Creative Industries: UK Television Exports Inquiry*, HMSO. http://www.culture.gov.uk

DCMS (2000), *Creative Industries: Out of the Box*, HMSO. http://www.culture.gov.uk

DCMS (2001), 'Banking on a hit: the funding dilemma for Britain's music businesses'. http://www.culture.gov.uk/global/publications/archive_2001/default.htm

DCMS (2004), 'Facts and figures'. http://www.culture.gov.uk/broadcasting/default.htm

Digital-Lifestyles (2004), 'Providing the fuel for a creative nation: an interview with Paula Le Dieu, Joint Director on the BBC Creative Archive', 28 May. http://www.digital-lifestyles.info/display_page.asp?section=cm&search=1&id=1263

Doctorov, C. (2002), 'The street finds its own use for the law of unintended consequences'. http://www.oreillynet.com/pub/a/network/2002/04/16/cory.html 04/16/2002

Drahos, P. (1996), *A Philosophy of Intellectual Property*, Aldershot: Dartmouth Publishing.

Drahos, P. and J. Braithwaite (2002), *Information Feudalism: Who Owns the Knowledge Economy?*, London: Earthscan.

The Economist (2002), 'Texting the television'. http://www.economist.com/business/displayStory.cfm?story_id=1392699

Fallenbock, M. (2002), 'On the Technical Protection of Copyright: The Digital Millennium Copyright Act, the European Community Copyright Directive and Their Anticircumvention Provisions', *International Journal of Communication Law and Policy*, 7 (Winter 2002/2003): 1–60.

Frith, S. (ed.) (1993), *Music and Copyright*, Edinburgh: Edinburgh University Press.

Frith, S. (2004), 'Music and the Media', in S. Frith, and L. Marshall (eds), *Music and Copyright*, 2nd edn, Edinburgh: Edinburgh University Press, pp. 171–88.

Geitner, P. (2004), '36 per cent of software sold last year was pirated: survey', *CNews*, 7 July. http://cnews.canoe.ca/CNEWS/TechNews/BizTech/2004/07/07/528382-ap.html

Gibson, O. (2002), 'Bazalgette hits out at TV "tsars"', *Media Guardian*, 22 October.

Goodwin, A. (1990), 'Sample and Hold: Pop Music in the Digital Age of Reproduction', in S. Frith and A. Goodwin (eds), *On Record: Rock, Pop and the Written Word*, London: Routledge, pp. 258–73.

Greenfield, S. and G. Osborne (2004), 'Copyright Law and Power in the Music Industry', in S. Frith, and L. Marshall (eds), *Music and Copyright*, 2nd edn, Edinburgh: Edinburgh University Press, pp. 88–102.

The Guardian (2004), 'Encrypted DVD may avoid Oscars' screener row', 17 June.

Harris, L. E. (1998), *Digital Property: Currency of the 21st Century*, New York: McGraw-Hill Ryerson.

Haynes, R. (1999), "'There's many a slip' twixt the eye and the lip": An Exploratory History of Football Broadcasts and Running Commentaries from 1927–39', *International Review for the Sociology of Sport*, 32 (2): 143–56.

Hebdige, D. (1979), *Subculture: The Meaning of Style*, London: Methuen.

Horsman, M. (1997), *Sky High: The Rise and Rise of BSkyB*, London: Texere Publishing.

Horsman, M. (2003), 'An answer to independents' prayers', *Financial Times*, *Creative Business*, 8 July.

Howkins, J. (2001), *The Creative Economy: How People Make Money from Ideas*, London: Penguin Books.

Hylton, J. G. (2001), 'Baseball Cards and the Birth of the Right of Publicity: The Curious Case of Haelean Laboratories v Topps Chewing Gum', *Marquette Sports Law Review*, 12: 273–85.

ITC (2002a), *Code on Sports and Other Listed Events*, published by Ofcom. http://www.ofcom.org.uk/codes_guidelines/broadcasting/tv/eco_reg_comp_pub/code_sprt_lstd_evts/?a=87101

ITC (2002b), *A Review of the UK Programme Supply Market*. http://www.ofcom.org.uk

Laing, S. (1993), 'Copyright and the International Music Industry', in S. Frith (ed.), *Music and Copyright*, Edinburgh: Edinburgh University Press, pp. 22–39.

Lane, S. (1999), 'The Problems of Personality Merchandising in English Law: The King, the Princess, and the Penguins', in E. Barendt et al., *The Yearbook of Copyright and Media Law 1999*, Oxford: Oxford University Press, pp. 28–65.

Lessig, L. (1999), *Code and Other Laws of Cyberspace*, New York: Basic Books.

Lessig, L. (2001), *The Future of Ideas: The Fate of the Commons in a Connected World*, New York: Random House.

Lessig, L. (2004), *Free Culture: How Big Media Uses Technology and the Law to Lock Down Culture and Control Creativity*, New York: Penguin Books.

Litman, J. (2001), *Digital Copyright*, Amherst: Prometheus Books.

Locke, J. (1988), *Two Treatises of Government*, Student Edition (Cambridge Texts in the History of Political Thought), ed. P. Laslett, Cambridge: Cambridge University Press.

McCarthy, J. T. and P. M. Anderson (2001), 'Protection of the Athlete's Identity: The Right of Publicity, Endorsements and Domain Names', *Marquette Sports Law Review*, 11: 195–209.

Madow, M. (1993), 'Private Ownership of Public Image: Popular Culture and Publicity Rights', *California Law Review*, 81: 125. http://www.cyberlaw.harvard.edu/propertyφφ/respect/madow.html

Marshall, L. (2002), 'Metallica and Morality: The Rhetorical Battleground of the Napster Wars', *Entertainment Law*, 1: 1–18.

Marshall, L. and S. Frith (2004), 'Afterword: Where Now for Copyright?', in S. Frith and L. Marshall (eds), *Music and Copyright*, 2nd edn, Edinburgh: Edinburgh University Press, pp. 1–20.

May, C. (2002), *The Information Society: A Sceptical View*, Cambridge: Polity Press.

Merriden, T. (2001), *Irresistible Forces: The Business Legacy of Napster and the Growth of the Underground Internet*, Oxford: Capstone.

Milmo, D. (2004), 'The hacker catchers', *The Guardian*, 4 August. http://media.guardian.co.uk/site/story/0,14173,1275374,00.html

National Academy of Sciences (2000), *The Digital Dilemma: Intellectual Property in the Information Age*, Washington, DC: National Academy Press. http://www.nap.edu/html/digital_dilemma/

National Research Council (2000), *The Digital Dilemma: Intellectual Property in the Information Age*, Washington, DC: National Academy Press.

National Statistics (2003), *International Service Transactions of the Film and Television Industries, 2002*. http://www.statistics.gov.uk

Naughton, J. (1999), *A Brief History of the Future: Origins and Destiny of the Internet*, London: Weidenfeld & Nicolson.

Naughton, J. (2004), 'A law unto themselves', *The Observer*, 13 June. http://observer.guardian.co.uk/business/story/0,6903,1237374,00.html

Negroponte, N. (1996), *Being Digital*, London: Coronet.

O'Brian, D. (2003), 'Auntie's digital revelation', *The Guardian*, 28 August.

Ofcom (2004), 'Outcome of appeal by The Number (UK) Ltd regarding complaint by David Bedford', *Advertising Complaints Bulletin*, 14 January. http://www.ofcom.org.uk/bulletins/adv_comp/content_board/?a=87101

Oliver, M. (2003), 'Former athlete to sue over directory ads', *The Guardian*, 6 October.

PACT (2004), 'Code of practice on BBC's dealings with independent producers for television programmes commissioned by the BBC'. http://www.pact.co.uk/uploads/file_bank/1211.doc

Passman, D. (2002), *All You Need to Know about the Music Business*, London: Penguin Books.

Pearce, M. (2004), 'An advert or the real thing?', *The Media Guardian*, 9 February.

Preston, A. (2002), *Risky Business: Inside the Indies*, Full Report, The Research Centre for Television and Interactivity. http://www.researchcentre.co.uk

Preston, A. (2003), *Inside the Commissioners*, The Research Centre for Television and Interactivity. http://www.researchcentre.co.uk

Puttnam, D. (1997), *Undeclared War: Struggle for Control of the World's Film Industry*, London: HarperCollins.

Robertson, G. and A. Nicol (1992), *Media Law*, London: Penguin.

Samualson, P. (1996), 'The Copyright Grab', *Wired*, January. http://www.wired.com/wired/archive/4.01/white.paper_pr.html

Samualson, P. (1997), 'Big Media Beaten Back', *Wired*, March. http://www.wired.com/wired/archive/5.03/netizen_pr.html

Sendall, B. (1982), *History of Independent Television in Britain: Origin and Foundation, 1946–62, Vol. 1*, London: Palgrave-Macmillan.

Shiva, V. (2001), *Protect or Plunder? Understanding Intellectual Property Rights*, London: Zed Books.

snopes.com (2002), 'Happy Birthday, We'll Sue'. http://www.snopes.com/music/songs/birthday.htm (accessed 30 July 2004).

Suthersanen, U. (2002), 'Napster, DVD and All That: Developing a Coherent Copyright Grid for Internet Entertainment', in E. Barendt et al., *The Yearbook of Copyright and Media Law 2002*, Oxford: Oxford University Press, pp. 207–50.

Taylor, M. and R. Towse (1998), 'The value of performers' rights: an economic approach', *Media, Culture and Society*, 20, 631–52.

Towse, R. (2004), 'Copyrights and Economics', in S. Frith and L. Marshall (eds), *Music and Copyright*, 2nd edn, Edinburgh: Edinburgh University Press, pp. 54–69.

Toynbee, J. (2004), 'Musicians', in S. Frith and L. Marshall (eds), *Music and Copyright*, 2nd edn, Edinburgh: Edinburgh University Press, pp. 123–38.

Vaidhyanathan, S. (2001), *Copyrights and Copywrongs: The Rise of Intellectual Property and How it Threatens Creativity*, New York: New York University Press.

Viljoen, D. (2003), *The Art of the Deal: Essential Guide to Business Affairs for Television and Film Producers*, 2nd edn, London: PACT Publications.

Waldman, S. (2003), 'At home with the Führer', *The Guardian*, 3 November.

Wallis, R. (2004), 'Copyright and the Composer', in S. Frith and L. Marshall (eds), *Music and Copyright*, 2nd edn, Edinburgh: Edinburgh University Press, pp. 103–22.

Walsh, A. and A. Brown (1999), *Not For Sale! Manchester United, Murdoch and the Defeat of BSkyB*, Edinburgh: Mainstream.

WTO (2004), 'What are intellectual property rights?' http://www.wto.org/english/tratop_e/trips_e/intel1_e.htm

Glossary

Advanced Audio Coding (AAC)

The new emerging standard of audio compression on the Internet that is more efficient than previous formats such as MP3 but retains the sound quality to rival that of CD audio. The audio codec, also referred to as MPEG-4, is used by Apple's iTunes software. (www.apple.com/mpeg4/aac/)

Alliance Against Counterfeiting and Piracy (AACP)

A trade organisation that seeks to inform and educate consumers about the dangers of media piracy. It commissions research to project the levels of counterfeiting and piracy to the public. (www.aacp.org.uk)

ARPANET

One of the original computer networks that eventually became known as the Internet. Formed in 1969 and used by the US military research unit called the Advanced Research Projects Administration (ARPA) during the Cold War. (en.wikipedia.org/wiki/ARPANET)

British Music Rights (BMR)

An umbrella organisation which represents the interests of composers, songwriters and music publishers. In the context of media rights, one of its stated aims is to promote 'An understanding of the rights and rewards for creativity in the music business and the value of those rights to the UK economy'. (www.bmr.org)

British Phonographic Industry (BPI)

The British music industry's main trade organisation, representing most of the UK's recording companies. Operates to fight piracy and to lobby politicians and the public on behalf of the industry. (www.bpi.co.uk)

CD-R

Stands for Compact Disc-Recordable. A type of media that allows you to record information using a CD recorder. Increasingly used by music fans to copy and share music. (CD-RW are rewritable discs.)

Communications Act 2003

Seminal media and communications legislation by the UK Labour government. Among its most important features for media rights is the creation of the regulator Ofcom and the retention of secondary rights by independent television producers under new terms of trade with broadcasters. (www.legislation.hmso.gov.uk/acts/acts2003/20030021.htm)

Copyright

The exclusive rights granted to authors to control and exploit their works within a certain timeframe. Often viewed as the key motivation to encourage creativity, a concept now hotly disputed.

Copyright, Designs and Patents Act 1988

The last major piece of legislation on copyright in the UK; however, it has received numerous revisions throughout the 1990s and more recently following the European Copyright Directive in 2001. (www.hmso.gov .uk/acts/acts1988/Ukpga_19880048_en_1.htm)

Creative Commons

An activist rights organisation and the administrator of 'creative commons licences' that enables artists, media producers, writers and other creatives to share their creations with the public with 'some rights reserved' or 'no rights reserved'. Run by the Berkman Center for Internet and Society at Stanford Law School through its figurehead Lawrence Lessig. CC licences are innovative ways of avoiding the prohibitive nature of strict copyright laws. (www.creativecommons.org)

Creative industries

Defined by the DCMS as 'those industries which have their origin in individual creativity, skill and talent and which have a potential for wealth and job creation through the generation and exploitation of intellectual property'. (www.culture.gov.uk/creative_industries/default.htm)

DeCSS

Devised by, among others, Norwegian teenager Jon Johansen, this is a computer code that enables its users to decrypt the Content Scrambling System (CSS), hence the 'de' prefix, to access content held on a DVD. Originally devised for Linux users whose computer drives were not licensed to play DVDs. (en.wikipedia.org/wiki/DeCSS)

Department of Culture, Media and Sport (DCMS)

The UK government's office in charge of policies for the arts, sport, broadcasting, film, the music industry and the press as well as other aspects of culture and cultural heritage. (www.culture.gov.uk)

Digital Millennium Copyright Act 1998 (DMCA)

The US government's most important legislation on copyright in the digital media environment. Introduced by the Clinton administration after intense lobbying by the US copyright industries, specifically the MPAA and RIAA, the new laws were used to prosecute the file-sharing service Napster and subsequently hundreds of individuals found to be illegally downloading high volumes of copyright material. (www.copyright.gov/legislation/dmca.pdf)

Digital Rights Management (DRM)

Increasingly used by the media industries as a way of technologically protecting digital media content from being accessed, copied, distributed or manipulated without the consent of the copyright holder. Includes watermarking and encryption technologies.

Digital Versatile Disc (DVD)

The audio-visual industry's standard carrier for storing and distributing television programmes and films to the consumer. DVDs provide higher video and sound quality and are the fastest-growing media technology in history. Their most contentious feature is their regional licensing system and encryption to prevent copying.

Digitalisation

Widely referred-to process of the media's movement from largely analogue forms of production, distribution and consumption to predominantly digital modes of communication. The binary codes of digital media mean that content is easier to manipulate and, crucially in the context of copyright, to copy.

European Broadcasting Union (EBU)

Founded in 1950 by newly emerging broadcasters as a pan-European trade association, the EBU has acted as a central distributor of broadcast rights to sport and other programming since the mid-1950s. This has included rights to the football World Cup (from 1954 to 1994) and the Olympic Games (from 1956 to 2004). With its administrative centre in Switzerland, the EBU has seventy-two member organisations. (www.ebu.ch/en/)

European Copyright Directive 2001 (ECD)

Directive 2001/29/EC of the European Parliament and of the Council of 22 May 2001 on the harmonisation of certain aspects of copyright and related rights in the information society. One of the most hotly disputed pieces of legislation in the EU's history. Introduced anti-circumvention protection for the first time. (europa.eu.int/information_society/topics/multi/digital_rights/doc/directive_copyright_en.pdf)

Freedom of information

Recent legislation in the UK and in many European nations recognises the demands of citizens to have greater public access to information about the workings of public bodies and government. In the age of the Internet, information is potentially more readily accessible than ever before, and legislation like the Freedom of Information Act 2000 ensures that public organisations are more 'open' and responsive to these needs. The Act gives broad rights: the right to be told whether certain information exists and the right to receive the information.

Image right

Broadly defined as the commercial appropriation of someone's personality, including indices of their image, voice, name and signature.

Intangible property

Defined as property with no physical presence. It is a form of property that derives value not from its intrinsic physical nature but from what it represents. Copyright, trademarks, patents and trade secrets are viewed as being intangible in this context.

Intellectual property (IP)

WIPO defines IP as 'products of the mind: inventions, literary and artistic works, any symbols, names, images and designs used in commerce'. In fact, the term more broadly represents a collection of proprietary rights that protect creations from computer software to pharmaceuticals.

Interactive television (iTV)

With the development of digital or high-definition television (HDTV), viewers are now able to interact with television services through their remote control. Broadcasters and programme makers are now building interactive content into their services to enable viewers to capture information, view multiple screens through one channel and communicate through their television sets. These developments have concurrent implications for rights owners, such as sports organisations, that can sell additional licences for broadcasters to produce such content.

International Federation of Phonographic Industries (IFPI)

An international trade organisation for the music industry that, as well as promoting the interests of the recording industry, is heavily involved in anti-piracy campaigns and lobbying governments and global media organisations. (www.ifpi.org/)

iTunes/iPod

Apple Computer's music archive software and music download service. Available for both Mac and PC users, the software services the commercial development of Apple's innovative digital music player, the iPod, fast becoming the *de facto* standard in portable digital-music consumption. (www.apple.com/itunes/)

Knowledge economy

This phrase, a buzzword during the formative years of e-commerce and the dotcom boom in the late 1990s, refers to the process whereby knowledge-based or information-based industries are replacing and far outweighing classic economies based on labour and capital. It suggests that economic growth is driven by the accumulation of knowledge.

Licence/Licensing

The contractual agreement granting permission to use intellectual property rights under agreed conditions. Licences might include the rights to make, use, reproduce, sell or import material that is in copyright or has a registered trademark.

Listed events

A list of designated live broadcasts from sporting events protected by UK legislation to ensure that they appear on free-to-air television and cannot be sold on an exclusive basis to pay-TV broadcasters. Listed events are also protected under the EC directive *Television Without Frontiers*.

Mechanical Copyright Protection Society (MCPS)

Collecting society that collects and distributes 'mechanical' royalties generated from recording music in different formats. (www.mcps.co.uk)

Media rights

The range of intellectual property rights and contractual rights that underpin the economic and commercial operation of the media industries.

Moral rights

The Berne Convention first recognised that authors have a paternity right in the work they create to enable them to prevent distortion or alteration of their work. The author's non-economic rights – their honour and reputation – are held in perpetuity by the original author and are non-transferable. Otherwise referred to as *Droit moral* due to their French origins. (www.intellectual-property.gov.uk/std/faq/copyright/moral_rights .htm)

Motion Picture Association of America (MPAA)

The trade association that operates on behalf of the US television and movie industry. One of the strongest lobby groups in the regulation of global piracy of audio-visual content. (www.mpaa.org)

Napster

The first peer-to-peer file-sharing technology that gained mass appeal for users to download MP3 files. Devised by programmer Shawn Fanning.

After a lawsuit by the RIAA, Napster closed down in 2002 and then re-emerged in 2004 as a legitimate music download service owned by Roxio, a leading software company.

Ofcom

The UK's Office of Communication was established under the Communication Act 2003 and took over the responsibilities of previous industry regulators the Independent Television Commission, the Broadcasting Standards Commission, the Radio Authority, Oftel and the Radiocommunications Agency. Ofcom was introduced to regulate the media in the age of advanced digital networks and telecommunications. (www.ofcom.org.uk)

Passing off

Tort preventing a person or organisation from representing the marks, packaging or identifying features of goods and services of another as their own. Increasingly used in the protection of image rights of celebrities as a way of recognising their commercial rights and goodwill associated with their name.

Patent

A monopoly right sanctioned by the state to a creator of an invention to exclude others from copying and exploiting the creation. (www.patent.gov.uk)

Peer-to-peer (P2P)

A network that is not based on the client/service-provider model of the Internet but is made up of peer nodes that function as both clients and servers. P2P essentially enables users to share files and retrieve information held on other computers on the network. (www.openp2p.com)

Performing Artists' Media Rights Association (PAMRA)

A collecting agency working on behalf of performers – both featured and non-featured – to collect and distribute royalties from recorded performances of music across all media outlets. (www.pamra.org.uk)

Performing Right Society (PRS)

A UK collecting agency for the collection and distribution of rights in performance for music artists and publishers. This includes any public

performance or broadcast of a work, including via the Internet. (www.prs
.co.uk)

Phonographic Performance Limited (PPL)

A collecting society for record companies and performers that licenses
music use by broadcasters, leisure and catering facilities, shops, nightclubs
and bars. (www.ppluk.com)

Piracy

A morally loaded term used by the copyright industries to refer to
the illegitimate use of media content. The word is confusingly used to
encompass illegal manufacture, distribution and sale of media content
as well as non-commercial reproductions of media content, including
peer-to-peer file-sharing and home copying, which are frequently viewed
as criminal behaviour. As digital technologies change and develop, so
too does the meaning of piracy and the range of behaviour it covers.
(www.piracyisacrime.com/)

Public domain

A work openly available to everyone and not subject to copyright protection is said to be in the public domain. Public-domain works are considered part of our cultural heritage, and anyone can use and build upon
them without restriction. Works are in the public domain either because
copyright in them has expired or because they are of a factual nature and
pertain to real events and people. (www.law.duke.edu/cspd/)

Recording Industry Association of America (RIAA)

A trade group that represents the US recording industry. It states that
its mission is to 'foster a business and legal climate that supports and
promotes our members' creative and financial vitality'. The RIAA is
the organisation that has brought lawsuits against peer-to-peer networks, most famously Napster, and in 2004 had prosecuted more than
5,000 individuals considered to be serious illegal downloaders. (www.riaa-
.com)

Rental Directive 1992

The 1992 Council Directive on the Rental and Lending Right and Certain Related Rights gives authors, performing artists and producers of
films and phonograms an exclusive right to authorise or to prohibit the

rental or lending of their works and productions. (europa.eu.int/ISPO/
ecommerce/legal/documents/392L0100/392L0100_EN.doc)

Secondary rights

Otherwise variously described as tertiary rights, ancillary rights or spin-
off rights. These rights usually pertain to the film and television industries
and cover such things as the licensing of publishing rights (based on a
production or series), merchandising rights, soundtrack rights and format
rights.

Serial Copying Management System (SCMS)

The Serial Copying Management System was forced on the hardware developers by the software manufacturers (i.e. record companies) to prevent
unlimited digital copying of CDs and other prerecorded media.

Sport–TV nexus

A term used to explain the symbiotic relationship between the sport and
television industries.

Trademark

A distinctive word, phrase, logo, domain name, graphic symbol, slogan
or other device that is used to identify the source of a product and to dis-
tinguish one manufacturer's products from another's. Trademarks must
be registered to be effective. (www.patent.gov.uk/tm/)

TRIPS

Trade-Related Aspects of Intellectual Property Rights is a multilateral
international treaty that attempts to provide a common set of laws on
intellectual property around the world. It has been heavily criticised for
benefiting the leading industrialised nations and producing unfair competition in both local and global markets. It is administered by the World
Trade Organisation. (www.wto.org/english/tratop_e/trips_e/trips_e.htm)

TV formats

One of the most rapidly expanding areas of television production,
referring to the rights associated with a written or visual expression of a

programme idea that either has already been made or can be adapted to the local market.

World Intellectual Property Organisation (WIPO)

Based in Geneva, Switzerland, this is the major international organisation for the promotion of intellectual property. As one of the specialist agencies of the United Nations, WIPO administers international treaties such as the Berne Convention and is also host to the Domain Name Resolution Service, the arbitrator of cybersquatting cases. (www.wipo.int)

World Trade Organisation (WTO)

The global international organisation dealing with the rules of trade between nations of which intellectual property rights are a major component. (www.wto.org)

Index

A Cinderella Story, 131
access-circumvention, 38
Acts
  Audio Home Recording Act (1998), 63
  Broadcasting Act (1990), 76, 92
  Broadcasting Act (1996), 76–7
  Communications Act (2003), 8, 19, 91, 95
  Copyright, Designs and Patent Act (1988), 13
  Copyright and Related Rights Regulations (2003) (Sonny Bono Act), 27
  Digital Millennium Copyright Act (1998) (DMCA), 37–9, 121
  EC Rental Directive (92/100/EEC), 51
  EC E-Commerce Directive (00/31/EC), 121
  EC IPR Enforcement Directive (2004), 121
  EU Copyright Directive (2001/29/EC), 27–8
  Fairness in Music Licensing Act (1998), 51
Alliance Against Counterfeiting and Piracy (AACP), 134
Amstrad, 18–19
Australian Competition and Consumer Commission (ACCC), 26
Azmi, Ida, 128

Barnett, Steve, 76
BBC, 126, 141–2; *see also* sports broadcasting rights
Beckham, David, 8
Bedford, David, 107–9
Berne Convention, 21–2, 49, 118
Berners-Lee, Tim, 116
Beverley-Smith, Hugh, 102, 103
Big Brother, 7, 96–8
Bob the Builder, 87
Booth, Jenny, 139

Bowman, Lisa M., 40
Boyle, James, 16, 38–9, 113, 138–9
Braithwaite, John, 10, 15–16, 24–5, 107, 132
Branscomb, Anne Wells, 117
breech of confidence, 110
British Pathe Film Archive, 141
Brook, David, 98
BSkyB, 6; *see also* sports broadcasting rights
BT, 129
Business Software Alliance, 28–9

Campbell, Naomi (v *Daily Mirror*), 110
Canal Plus Technologies, 35–7
Carlton Communications, 34
Castells, Manual, 125
celebrity, 102–3
commons, the, 136–42
  enclosure, 113–14
Content Scrambling System (CSS), 33, 39–40
Coombe, Rosemary, 102
copy-circumvention, 18
copyleft, 137
copyright
  bundle of rights, 17–19
  duration, 19–20
  EU directives, 26–28
  ideas/expression dichotomy, 14, 17
  internationalisation, 21–5
  ownership of ideas, 10
Copyright Coalition on Domain Names, 128
Correa, Carlos, 24
Creative Commons (CC), 140–1
creative economy, 9
Creative Industries Task Force, 88–91

DeCCS, 39–41
'digital dilemma', 5, 31
digital rights management (DRM), 33–7, 59

digital television, 84–5
    ITV Digital, 6, 34–5, 73–4
digitalisation, 31–3
Doctorov, Cory, 131, 140
domain names *see* Internet and trademark
Drahos, Peter, 10, 15–16, 24–5, 101, 132
DVD, 32–3, 39–41

Eldred v Ashcroft, 20–1
Endemol, 96

fair dealing (fair use), 41–2
false endorsement, 107
Federation Against Copyright Theft (FACT), 134
formats (TV), 95–8
Frith, Simon, 55, 140

'gift economy', 137
Granada Television, 34
Greenfield, Steve, 135

Haelean Labs v Topps Chewing Gum, 105
Harris, Lesley Ellen, 34
Harry Potter and the Prisoner of Azkaban, 135
Hebdige, Dick, 58
Hitler, Adolph, 3–4
Homes and Gardens, 3–4
Horsman, Matthew, 94
Howkins, John, 9, 125
Hugo, Victor, 21

ICANN, 126–7
iCraveTV, 124
image rights, 8, 100–12
Independent Television Commission (ITC), 91–5
intellectual property (IP)
    influence on media, 9
    philosophy of, 14–17
International Federation of Phonogrammes Industries (IFPI), 55
International Music Joint Venture, 84
Internet
    as 'neutral network', 115–17
    and copyright, 117–25
    file sharing, 59–64
    hyperlinking, 122–5
    influence on media, 8
    safe harbours, 119–20
    trademarks, 127–8

IPC Media, 3
Irvine, Eddy v Talksport, 106–7

Johansen, John, 40
Jowell, Tessa, 84

Laddie, J., 107
Laing, Stuart, 55
Lane, Shelley, 100
Lessig, Lawrence, 8, 31, 33, 115, 132, 143
Litman, Jessica, 15, 38, 124
Locke, John, 16, 101

Madow, John, 102
Marshall, Lee, 56, 140
May, Christopher, 113, 137
media rights defined, 9
Microsoft, 114
Moore, Michael, 131
Motion Picture Association of America (MPPA), 27
music
    basket of rights, 49
    collecting societies, 49–56
    copyright infringement, 55–64
    history, 48–9
    iTunes, 65
    measurement of use, 53
    mechanical rights, 51–2
    Michael, George, 139
    MP3, 30–2, 64
    MyMP3.com, 61
    Napster, 11, 61–2
    neighbouring rights, 52–3
    performance rights, 50–1
    Recording Industry Association of America (RIAA), 61–2
    Serial Copy Management System (SCMS), 58
    tape levy, 57

Narowzian v Arks Limited and others, 17
National Academy of Sciences, 5
Naughton, John, 114, 125
NDS, 35–7
Negroponte, Nicholas, 31
News Corporation, 35–6
Nicol, Andrew, 18

O'Brian, Danny, 142
Office of Communications (Ofcom), 94–5, 108
OnDigital *see* ITV Digital
open source, 137–8
Osborne, Guy, 135

parallel imports, 25–6
passing off, 106–9
performance rights, 50–1
piracy, 35, 133–6
Presley, Elvis, 104
Princess of Wales, 105
privacy, 109–11
Producers' Alliance for Cinema and
    Television (PACT), 93–4
Puttnam, David, 88

recordable compact discs (CD-R),
    56–9
Religious Technology Centre v Netcom
    Online Communications Services,
    120–1
right of publicity, 103, 105
Robertson, Graham, 18
Roman law, 13

set-top-box (STB), 35–7
Shetland Times v *Shetland News*,
    122
Shiva, Vandana, 23
Singin' in the Rain, 17
Spertus, James, 134
Spike TV, 105–6
sports broadcasting rights
    Attheraces, 79–82
    BBC, 72–3
    BSkyB, 70–2, 74–6, 79–82
    EC investigation of Premier League,
        74–5
    history, 68–71
    listed events, 6, 76–8
    Manchester United takeover, 72
    new media and, 78–82

Office of Fair Trading and sports
    rights, 72, 80–1
Tasini, Jonathan, 122–3
Suthersanen, Uma, 42

television exports, 85–7
terms of trade (independent producers),
    94–5
tertiary rights, 87
Thomas the Tank Engine, 87
321 Studios, 41
Towse, Ruth, 53
Toynbee, Jason, 64
Trade Related Aspects of Intellectual
    Property Rights (TRIPs), 22–3
trademark, 104–6

Universal City Studios v Sony
    Corporation ('Betamax Case'), 18, 62
Universal Copyright Convention, 22
Unix, 137
US hegemony, 7, 85–6

Vaidhyanathan, Siva, 8, 10, 134
Valenti, Jack, 12

Waldman, Simon, 3
warehousing, 93
Who Wants to be a Millionnaire?, 7
World Intellectual Property Organisation
    (WIPO), 22–4
    WIPO Copyright Treaty (1996), 37–9,
        118
World Trade Organisation, 22–3, 37
Wyman, Bill, 104

Zeta-Jones, Catherine v Hello, 110–11

EU Authorised Representative:

Easy Access System Europe Mustamäe tee 50, 10621 Tallinn, Estonia

gpsr.requests@easproject.com

Printed and bound by CPI Group (UK) Ltd, Croydon, CR0 4YY

09/06/2025

01897300-0001